THE ULTIMATE CRICUT BEGINNER'S GUIDE: 3 BOOKS IN 1

CRICUT FOR BEGINNERS+ MASTERING DESIGN SPACE+ TONS OF PROJECT IDEAS AND HOW TO MAKE MONEY WITH YOUR CRICUT (LATEST METHODS) + 3 AMAZING BONUSES THAT WILL SAVE YOU TONS OF TIME AND MONEY.

KEREN DEANS

© Copyright 2021 - All rights reserved.

It is not legal to reproduce, duplicate, or transmit any part of this document in either electronic means or in printed format. Recording of this publication is strictly prohibited and any storage of this document is not allowed unless with written permission from the publisher except for the use of brief quotations in a book review.

CONTENTS

BOOK 1
Cricut for Beginners, 2021 and Beyond: The Fast-and-Easy Beginner's Guide to Becoming a Cricut Master

Claim Your Bonus	9
Introduction	11
1. CRICUT 101: EVERYTHING YOU NEED TO KNOW ABOUT CRICUT MACHINES	13
What is a Cricut machine?	13
Cricut machine models	14
Which one should I get?	23
What projects can I do with the Cricut machine?	27
2. ALL YOU NEED TO KNOW ABOUT CRICUT TOOLS AND ACCESSORIES	37
Blades & tools and their functions	37
Pens & Markers	50
Art Supplies & Accessories	58
3. MATERIALS: WHAT CAN I CUT WITH MY CRICUT MAKER OR CRICUT EXPLORE SERIES?	68
Cricut Explore series - Compatible materials	69
Cricut Maker - Compatible materials	73
4. HOW TO MAINTAIN YOUR CRICUT	81
Cleaning your Cricut machine	81
Re-greasing your Cricut machine	82
How to maintain your Cricut mats	83
Maintaining your Cricut blades	87
Conclusion	91
References	93

BOOK 2
Cricut Design Space for 2021 and Beyond: The Beginner's Step-by-Step Guide to Mastering Cricut Design Space in Just 21 Days

Claim Your Bonus	101
Introduction	103
1. DESIGN SPACE AND HOW TO LAUNCH IT	105
Downloading, Installing, and Launching Design Space on:	105
Windows PC	105
Mac PC	107
iOS	110
Android Device	112
Uninstall Cricut Design Space	114
Unwrap and Set Up Your Newly Purchased Cricut Machine	116
Cricut Access	118
Cricut Access Plans	119
Difference Between Cricut Access, Cricut Cartridges, Licensed Fonts, and Images	122
Alternative Options for Cricut Access	123
2. MASTERING THE DESIGN SPACE CANVAS AREA	124
What exactly is the Canvas Area?	124
The Cricut Design Space Top Panel	125
Editing Menu	126
Left Panel	134
Right Panel	135
3. PROJECTS IN DESIGN SPACE	139
Saving, Opening, and Editing Design Space Project on:	139
Desktop	139
App	141
Sharing Your Design Space Project on:	143
iOS	143
Desktop	144
Use Design Space Templates	146
Use Ready-to-Make Design Space Projects	147
Use the Attach Tool	149
4. USING IMAGES IN DESIGN SPACE	151
Browse and Search for Cartridges	152
Search for Cartridges with a Filter	154
Download Cricut Cartridge Online	157

Purchasing Images on Cricut Design Space	157
Mac or Windows PC	157
iOS	159
Android Device	159
Uploading Images into Design Space	161
PC	162
iOS	166
Android Device	171
Use the Slice Tool to Edit Your Cricut Images	173
Edit Your Images in Upload Mode	175
Create Layers and Separate Objects	176
5. USEFUL TIPS IN ADVANCED DESIGN SPACE	181
Design Canvas Tips	181
Cut Screen Tips	190
6. CRICUT HACKS	200
Conclusion	227
References	229

BOOK 3
Cricut Project and Profit Ideas for 2021 and Beyond: The Beginner's Step-by-Step Guide to Tons of Project Ideas and Making Money Fast with Cricut

Claim Your Bonus	233
Introduction	235
1. CRICUT PROJECT IDEAS AND THEIR MATERIALS	237
Paper Crafting Ideas	237
Vinyl Craft Project Ideas	242
Heat Transfer Project Ideas	249
Fabric Craft Ideas	253
Cricut Infusible Ink Project Ideas	258
Best Cricut Crafts to Sell	259
2. A STEP-BY-STEP GUIDE FOR CRICUT PROJECTS	261
DIY Greeting Card	261
DIY Label	262
Vinyl on Mugs	264
Iron-On T-Shirt	265
Iron-On Adoption Banner	266

Paper Butterfly Heart	267
Infusible Ink Layered T-shirt	269
DIY Giant Paper Flower	271
DIY Valentine's Day Wreath	273
Cupcake Wrappers with Flowers	274
Spiderweb Garland	275
DIY Flower Art Napkin Ring	276
3D Candy Cart	277
3D Hot Air Balloon	279
Mini Halloween Treat Bags	280
3. MAKE MONEY WITH CRICUT	282
Profitable Cricut Projects to Sell	286
Market Your Cricut Projects	287
Conclusion	289
References	291

BOOK 1

CRICUT FOR BEGINNERS, 2021 AND BEYOND: THE FAST-AND-EASY BEGINNER'S GUIDE TO BECOMING A CRICUT MASTER

© Copyright 2021 - All rights reserved.

It is not legal to reproduce, duplicate, or transmit any part of this document in either electronic means or in printed format. Recording of this publication is strictly prohibited and any storage of this document is not allowed unless with written permission from the publisher except for the use of brief quotations in a book review.

CLAIM YOUR BONUS

The Cricut Tool Kit
This is what you'll get in this Free tool kit:

1. Over 100 beautiful **SVG Files** that will spark your creativity

2. The Cricut Supplies Cheatsheet, with the most essential supplies you'll need for your first project

3. Access to our private Facebook group where you get to meet like-minded Cricut lovers and get tons of project ideas and tons of **free SVGs**

To claim your tool kit simply <u>Click Here</u>. Or Copy and paste this link into your browser: https://productiveplans.activehosted.com/f/7

INTRODUCTION

What if I tell you that you have not been doing DIY arts and crafts the best way you should? You're gifted and enjoy doing DIY arts and crafts. You may be a small business entrepreneur who creates and sells beautiful artwork. But you spend a lot of time tracing and cutting that it may take up to a day to complete one piece of artwork.

What if I tell you that you've spent way too much time and effort in preparing your arts and crafts pieces? While there's an undeniable sense of comfort and solace in the process of creating these pieces, you're actually not doing them in the most efficient way possible.

Arts and crafts take a lot of dedication and effort, and artists will never compromise their quality.

However, it becomes a challenge when you have to use different materials, especially if you have to cut them by hand. Imagine how difficult it is to cut a tough piece of leather for a handmade wristband. You have to be extra careful with the scissors or blade so you won't make a crooked cut or, worse, cut your fingers. Or what if you have to cut a piece of tulle for a flower beret? Many crafters like tulle because it's a beautiful and dainty fabric, but it can be a pain to work with. You have to have a steady hand to cut this delicate material, and you can't be too rough with the scissors lest you tear it.

So, wouldn't it be great if there's something to help you save up to 60% of your time? Wouldn't it be great if you can do more in a day and increase your output?

If you own something that can produce similar factory-precision results for all your materials, imagine how much time you can save!

Not only think of how much time you can save with this kind of machine, but also the many different types of uniform cuts you can get on all your materials. This way, your work, even though handmade and unique, can still have the look and standard of something made on a commercial scale.

With this machine, not only you can cut delicate materials such as tulle or crepe paper, but you're also able to cut thick materials such as leather and even wood. As an artisan, I'm sure right now your mind is already running with all the things you want to and can create with a Cricut machine!

So, I'm here to share something that will change the way you do and look at arts and crafts. Yes, you guessed it, it's the glorious Cricut.

I'm going to help you with everything you need to know about a Cricut machine every step of the way!

And this means *everything* from A – Z.

You'll learn the right way to use a Cricut machine, you'll learn about what materials you can cut, and I'll even throw in some design ideas and inspirations to help you get started. I'll show you how to work the Cricut machine using different materials and what you can create with these materials.

Finally, I will show you the ways and practices to maintain your Cricut machine. A Cricut machine is not cheap, and you'll need to know the right and proper way to maintain it.

We'll start with an in-depth look at what a Cricut machine is in the first chapter. This chapter will show you all about the different types of Cricut machines and what each is used for. It's super essential for you to understand the difference since it can help you choose the right Cricut model better.

Are you excited already? I bet you are because I sure am!

So, get your felt, leather, and vinyl ready because you're in for a fun artsy ride!

1

CRICUT 101: EVERYTHING YOU NEED TO KNOW ABOUT CRICUT MACHINES

The Cricut machine has been around for more than 15 years. It has many great functions that crafters love, but not many of them own one. In this book, you'll learn why you should own a Cricut machine.

I've briefly talked about the Cricut machine in the introduction, and I hope I have piqued your interest.

So, what is about this machine that I love so much that I believe I can't live without it?

The Cricut machine, to me, is one of the best inventions. Therefore, in the chapters to come, we'll take an up-close and personal look at what makes this machine a wonderful piece of equipment.

Without further ado, let's take a look at what a Cricut machine is and what you can do with it.

WHAT IS A CRICUT MACHINE?

A Cricut machine is a type of cutting plotter machine designed for home crafters. To use a Cricut machine, you need to hook it up to your computer or smartphone. This way, the machine can detect the design from the design software you have on your device.

A Cricut machine can cut various types of common materials among home crafters such as leather, cardstock, vinyl, fabric, or even thin wood. Its blade provides accurate cuts on these materials, so you'll get precise designs all the time. The ability to cut many different types of materials means you're able to create various projects in the most creative ways possible.

Before your Cricut machine can cut your desired designs, you need to create one in the software. You can either create something of your own or use the software's readily available motifs and patterns. The design software has many beautiful and cool options you can choose from, so you'll never run out of ideas!

14 | BOOK 1

Once you've created or loaded the design into the software, your Cricut machine will cut them onto the material of your choice. The Cricut machine design software is free, and it's compatible with Windows, Mac, or smartphones, so you can work on the software no matter what your device is.

Since it was first designed and made for home crafters, the Cricut machine is straightforward to use and highly user-friendly. Even if you've never used a Cricut machine before, learning how to use it is often as easy as 1,2,3 because basically, that's all it takes!

1. Create your project designs in the software
2. Place your material onto the cutting mat and load it into the Cricut machine
3. Import your design and press the Start button to cut

That's it!

CRICUT MACHINE MODELS

Currently, there are several types of Cricut machine models available in the market. While these machines get the job done, it's essential to know the different models so you can make a better choice about which one will suit you best.

Let's take a closer look at these models to learn more. I'll share brief information and details about each model, but you can find the summary at the end of this section.

Cricut Joy (March 21st, 2020)

This mini Cricut machine is dubbed "Your DIY Best Friend." But don't let its size fool you because the Cricut Joy is a powerhouse in its own right.

1 - The compact but powerful Cricut Joy Photo via: Cricut Joy

You can use this latest model in the market for quick everyday projects such as to cut iron-on transfers for kid's t-shirts or make one of those fun peel-and-stick sticker labels for your spice jars. The Cricut Joy is perfect for those last-minute designs because you can quickly import a design from your smartphone, load your material, and voila, your project is ready within seconds!

If you love DIY arts and crafts but don't have a dedicated crafting space, then Cricut Joy is your solution. It fits easily in a drawer or a box that you don't have to worry about storage.

2 - Cricut Joy is space-saving & perfect for those with limited crafting area Photo via: Cricut Inspiration

This Cricut machine model can also write, draw, or doodle any design onto any material. You can choose different colors, fonts, or line weights, and the Cricut Joy will transfer the designs onto your fabric. This function works great if you want to create a unique monogram for your journals or even create handwritten-like designs on custom cards.

Even though the Cricut Joy can only cut materials up to 5.5 inches in width, it still does the job effortlessly and seamlessly. Despite its small size, the Cricut Joy can cut more than 50 different types of materials!

This model is perfect when you need to cut small designs because you don't have to get your full-size Cricut machine out. Even so, the Cricut Joy can cut one image up to 4.5 inches, and it's powerful enough to perform repeated cuts on materials that are up to 20 feet long.

Cricut Explore Air™ 2 (October 5th, 2016)

This 2016 model is a favorite among many crafters, making the Explore Air™ 2 the most popular model.

3 - Crafters' favorite Cricut machine Photo via: Cricut Inspiration

This elite model can cut more than 100 different material types at half the time than other Cricut machine models could. One of the best features on the Explore Air™ 2 model is the Fast Mode 2x Speed Feature. This function allows you to cut and write up to two times faster than previous Cricut models.

Even though Explore Air™ 2 can cut more than 100 various materials, the Fast Mode will not work on all fabrics. To know which material you can use Fast Mode on, you can choose your material from the dropdown list on your Cut screen. If you're using compatible material, the Fast Mode option will appear so you can choose to activate the mode or not. However, the Fast Mode is available on common materials such as cardstock, vinyl, and iron-on transfer.

You can use the Explore Air™ 2 to cut a design of up to 12 inches, and you can use it to make repeated cuts on materials up to 2 feet long. This model comes with 4 tools to switch and use for cutting, writing, or scoring.

Additionally, to suit different designers' colorful and fun personalities, the Cricut Explore Air™ 2 comes in 8 bright and bold colors! Other than the classic Mint or Black, you're also spoiled for choice because you can choose the Explore Air™ 2 in Boysenberry, Cobalt, Fuchsia, Merlot, Peacock, Persimmon, Raspberry, or Sunflower.

Cricut Explore Air (2014)

This was one of the earliest die-cutting machines made by Cricut.

5 - Many designers and crafters swear by Cricut thanks to its classic Cricut Explore Air Photo via: Amazon

Even though Cricut is no longer producing the Explore Air, I would like to highlight this model because there are still many Explore Air out there in the market. While you may find some pre-loved units, it's still an excellent machine to have if you want to save time on your arts and crafts projects.

This was the first Cricut model that came with a dual holder. Compared to the more popular Cricut Explore Air™ 2, the Explore Air doesn't come with the Fast Mode 2x speed feature. Having said that, other functions and features of these two machines are very similar. If you don't mind just a slightly longer waiting time while the Cricut Explore Air cuts your material, then this machine is still an excellent choice for any serious DIY crafters.

Despite being the earlier version of the Explore Air(™) 2, the Explore Air can still cut more than 100 different materials. With the Explore Air, you can cut vinyl, cardstocks of different weights, poster board, adhesive-backed cork, aluminum foil, and duct tape sheet.

Cricut Explore One (May 6th, 2015)

There are many Cricut machines in the current market, and there have been many models in the past. A discontinued Cricut machine is known as legacy machines.

The Cricut Explore One is a machine produced in 2015, and this classic Cricut is now one of the legacy machines. Even though the Cricut Explore One came out more than 6 years ago, it still works effortlessly and provides me with accurate cuts.

6 - 2015's Cricut Explore One model that's still loved by many Photo via: Cricut Pinterest

There are also still many Cricut Explore One available in the market. You can use it to make a wide range of DIY hobbies to cut, write, or score your materials. Just like its more contemporary counterparts, the Cricut Explore One can cut more than 100 materials.

Cricut Maker (August 20th, 2017)

The Cricut Maker is worth it. It's currently the top-of-the-line die-cutting machine, and I know many designers who couldn't live without theirs.

7 - The Cricut Maker is a must-have for pro designers Photo via: Cricut

I love this machine for its high strength cutting power as well as its pro-level functions. Among all the Cricut machines, the Maker can make laser-precise cuts on more than 300 materials. Not only that, it comes with an array of tools and blades to make all your pro designs a breeze.

The Knife Blade of the Cricut Maker can cut thick and dense materials such as chipboard or basswood. Other tools such as the Foil Transfer or Deboss tool adds a classy and sophisticated touch to your projects. The Cricut Maker is also highly versatile because you can easily change these tools at the touch of a button almost without any effort at all.

The Cricut Maker has more power and cutting strength with commercial-grade technology. This ability allows you to work with more materials, so there are more creative possibilities in the types of projects you can create. Whether it's creating a model for your kid's science project or cutting and marking your fabric for sewing projects, the Cricut Maker can handle almost anything.

Now that we've seen the Cricut models, both current and legacy machines, here's a quick summary of these five models:

	Cricut Joy	Explore Air™ 2	Maker	Explore Air	Explore One
Maximum material width	5.5"	12"	12"	12"	12"
Maximum material length	20'	2'	2'	2'	2'
Compatible materials	50+	100+	300+	100+	100+
Tools	2 Cutting and writing	4 Cutting, writing, and scoring	12 Cutting, writing, scoring, and other pro effects	4 Cutting, writing, and scoring	4 Cutting, writing, and scoring
Fast Mode	–	✓	✓	–	–
Long continuous cut without cutting mat	✓	–	–	–	–
Free design app (Windows, Android, Mac, and iOS)	✓	✓	✓	✓	✓

Other than models that can write, cut, or score, Cricut also has a range of fantastic heat presses known as the EasyPress™ series. These heat presses deliver better performance and more even heat transfer than your average iron.

While I'm somewhat used to transferring the designs on my items with an iron, I very much prefer to work with Cricut EasyPress™ because it provides an amazingly even heat transfer. Furthermore, the Cricut EasyPress™ Mini works perfectly when I need to transfer a design onto items that don't have flat surfaces, such as my kids' shoes or caps.

If you love working with heat transfer materials and have been struggling to get them to stay on your items, you'll love the Cricut EasyPress™. Here are the models available under the Cricut EasyPress™ series.

CRICUT 101: EVERYTHING YOU NEED TO KNOW ABOUT CRIC... | 19

Cricut EasyPress™ 2 (July 30th, 2018)

The EasyPress™ 2 is the updated and upgraded model from the Cricut EasyPress™. The machine provides good heat transfer and can cover a surface evenly. However, they're huge, and you need to place them on a specific table or designated area.

8 - EasyPress™ 2 is the perfect heat transfer for home crafters Photo via: Amazon

Cricut EasyPress™ 2 offers the same quality of heat transfer capability but with more mobility and freedom. You can carry the EasyPress™ 2 with you no matter where you are in your studio or home. Simply plug it in, wait 1 or 2 minutes for the element to heat up, and you're good to go!

Compared to the EasyPress™, the EasyPress™ 2 comes in three different sizes, which is perfect if you're looking for a heat press that suits your crafting needs. I own the EasyPress™, and it's rather bulky, and there were times I did resort to using an iron whenever I needed to heat transfer something small. So, I believe the three different size options in the EasyPress™ 2 range is a great solution.

9 - The Cricut EasyPress™ 2 range clockwise from left: Mid-Size, Jumbo, and Mini Photo via: Cricut Inspiration

Cricut EasyPress™ 2 capabilities based on size:

Small	Mid-size	Jumbo
6" x 7"	9" x 9"	12" x 10"
For small projects/items	For medium or everyday projects/items	For large projects/items
- Baby clothes	- Pillow covers	- Hoodies or sweaters
- Small bags	- Cushion covers	- Umbrellas
- Totes	- T-shirts	- Blankets
- Socks	- Bags	- Curtains
- Hats	- Aprons	- Banners

Cricut EasyPress™ 2 Mini (September 6th, 2019)

If I say that I wouldn't get another Cricut EasyPress™, I wasn't talking about the Cricut EasyPress™ 2 Mini!

10 - I love everything about the Cricut EasyPress™ 2 Mini! Photo via: Cricut

With a tagline of "Mini but mighty," you know you're in for something awesome.

It's a perfect heat press machine for anyone from beginners to experts. The size is petite and ergonomic, making it a really easy machine to handle. Most heat presses are cumbersome and require a lot of applied pressure from the user. It can also be very challenging to heat transfer items of odd sizes like hats or shoes using the conventional heat press.

With the EasyPress™ 2 Mini, you can manipulate, twist, and turn the press with ease. This versatility and mobility make the EasyPress™2 an excellent gadget to use when you need to heat transfer materials onto non-flat surfaces or hard-to-reach places.

However, because this is the mini version, it doesn't come with the temperature setting like other EasyPress™ models. Once you turn it on, you can set the EasyPress™ 2 Mini to three different heat settings i.e. low, medium, and high heat settings. Even without a temperature indicator, the heat settings are sufficient and can effectively transfer your designs onto your items.

11 - The EasyPress™ 2 Mini really is a wonderful invention Photo via: Cricut

But as you'd probably understand, we crafters need to know for certain as much as we can about our tools and craft. So, I got my husband's infrared thermometer to measure the temperature on each heat setting, and this is what I learned.

Heat Setting	Starting Temperature	Maximum Temperature
Low	252°F (122°C)	275°F (135°C)
Medium	283°F (139°C)	315°F (157°C)
High	365°F (185°C)	371°F (188°C)

Do note that this is a rough estimation, so there's room for error. As much as I've measured the temperature as close to the EasyPress™ 2 Mini plate, I know there's probably still some discrepancy from the exact temperature.

Even though I couldn't get the press up to 400°F, I don't find this to be a problem. The high setting can still transfer my design onto my items just as effectively as my EasyPress™ model.

Cricut EasyPress™ (August 2017)

Although the EasyPress™ only has one size, "9 x 9", it still does the job really well. This model has a lower maximum temperature than the EasyPress, so at times it doesn't transfer HTV that effectively because I have to press it for slightly longer. Having said that, it still can perform other heat transfer tasks well, so at the moment.

12 - The first EasyPress™ model from Cricut Photo via: Amazon

As mentioned earlier, compared to EasyPress™ 2, this model has a lower maximum temperature, which is 350°F (176°C). EasyPress™ 2, on the other hand, has a maximum temperature of 400°F (205°C). This means that EasyPress™ 2 does open up more possibilities to the projects you can create with heat transfer materials. This is because most heat transfer materials require at least 375°F, and certain heat transfer materials such as sublimation require 400°F.

However, if you don't usually work with very high-temperature heat transfer materials, the EasyPress™ is a fantastic Cricut heat transfer machine you can trust.

Here's a quick summary of the Cricut EasyPress™ series:

Features	EasyPress™ 2	EasyPress™ 2 Mini	EasyPress™
Size	6" x 7" 9" x 9" 12" x 10"	3.25" x 1.92"	9" x 9"
Color	Raspberry		Turquoise
Max. temperature	400°C (205°C)	371°F (188°C)	350°F (176°C)
USB Port	✓	-	-
Heat plate	Thicker		Thinner
Heat up time	25% faster		Fast
Remember last temperature	Yes	-	No
Sublimation	Yes	-	No

Overall, the Cricut EasyPress™ 2 is an impressive upgrade from the older version.

Other than the additional highly functional features, you can also upgrade the EasyPress™ firmware like you would for your phone or your computer software. If you have never owned a heat press before, I believe the Cricut EasyPress™ is a fantastic first investment.

WHICH ONE SHOULD I GET?

Now that you know the models made by Cricut (and probably excited for each one of them as I once was!), I understand that it could be challenging to decide which one would be the best one for you.

In the next section, I'll talk about each model's pros and cons. While this comparison is based on my personal experience, I believe it can help you make a better and more informed decision.

Project types & sizes

When it comes to Choosing the right Cricut, the most important thing to know before you get one is what you will need it for.

While all Cricut models are impressive, you should consider the capacity, size, and project types you usually do. Not only will these factors determine how effective your machine can deliver results, but it can also help manage your budget better.

As I've mentioned earlier, the EasyPress™ 2 series come in three different sizes, and there's also an option for a mini heat press. So, even if you've never worked with any heat transfer materials before or it's not a big part of your craft, having one handy is always a good idea.

To help you make a better decision, let's take a look at this general comparison table of Cricut machines and Cricut heat presses.

	Everyday DIY projects	Wide range of DIY projects & advanced hobby items	Pro-level / Commercial DIY projects & items
Cricut Joy	✓	–	–
Cricut Explore Air™ 2	✓	✓	–
Cricut Explore Air™	✓	✓	–
Cricut Explore One	✓	✓	–
Cricut Maker	✓	✓	✓
EasyPress™ 2	✓	✓	✓
EasyPress™ Mini	✓	–	–
EasyPress™	✓	✓	✓

Tools & capabilities

There are four main types of Cricut machine capabilities, i.e., cutting, writing, scoring, and pro-level effects. While you may not need every function, it still depends on each crafter regardless if they're producing designs on a small or a big scale.

All Cricut models can be used for writing and cutting. This means you can cut any design with any Cricut machine and also use the pen tool to write on your material. If you need extra features for your projects, such as scoring or other pro-level effects like foil transfer or perforation, then you'll need the more advanced model.

Currently, the most advanced Cricut model is the Cricut Maker. Not only it has more pro-level tools, but it can also cut thicker and denser materials because it has higher commercial-grade strength.

	Cutting & Writing only	Cutting, Writing & Scoring	Pro-level / Commercial DIY projects & items
Cricut Joy	✓	–	–
Cricut Explore Air™ 2	✓	✓	–
Cricut Explore Air™	✓	✓	–
Cricut Explore One	✓	✓	–
Cricut Maker	✓	✓	✓

	Everyday DIY projects	Wide range of DIY projects & advanced hobby items	Pro-level / Commercial DIY projects & items
EasyPress™ 2	✓	✓	✓
EasyPress™ Mini	✓	–	–
EasyPress™	✓	✓	✓

Material type & compatibility

While it's great to have a machine that can cut through virtually anything, it's still good to consider how often you are cutting these materials. Suppose you only need a Cricut machine for your daily DIY items or occasional decorative items. In that case, I believe you don't need one that can cut more than 300 different types of materials. The Cricut Explore Air™ 2 has material compatibility of up to 100+ materials, and this is already good enough for many crafters, both hobbyists, and serious ones.

Another thing you need to consider before getting a Cricut machine is the material width. Except for Cricut Joy, because of its small size, all Cricut models can cut materials with a width up to 12 inches. However, the Cricut Joy is the only model that can perform repeated and continuous cutting on a material that is 20 feet in length without the need for a cutting mat.

	50+ materials	100+ materials	300+ materials	Repeated/Continuous cutting
Cricut Joy	✓	–	–	✓
Cricut Explore Air™	✓	✓	–	–
Cricut Explore Air™	✓	✓	–	–
Cricut Explore One	✓	✓	–	–
Cricut Maker	✓	✓	✓	–

Connectivity

I love a Cricut machine's connectivity feature because I'm not limited to just a USB connection.

	Bluetooth®	USB
Cricut Joy	✓	–
Cricut Explore Air™ 2	✓	✓
Cricut Explore Air™	✓	✓
Cricut Explore One	✓ (Adapter sold separately)	✓
Cricut Maker	✓	✓

The wireless connectivity allows more mobility since I can choose to work wherever I am. Whether you prefer to be mobile or not, the connectivity feature is crucial because it gives you freedom whenever you require it.

It'll be both a shame and a waste if you only take out your Cricut machine during the festive seasons because you're not fully maximizing its potential. Having said that, you don't want to limit your creative potential by getting an underperforming Cricut machine.

So, consider your project size, usage frequency, tools you need, and the materials you work with most often before deciding on the right model.

WHAT PROJECTS CAN I DO WITH THE CRICUT MACHINE?

Wow, what *can't* you do with a Cricut machine!

At first, you may think that a Cricut machine only cuts things, and at the end of the day, there can't be *that* many things to cut. But having the Cricut machine means you're able to make incredible designs and cut fancy shapes without any effort at all. When you have all the cutouts or shapes you need, the only limit really is your imagination!

To give you an idea of just some of the things you can create, check out some of the projects that I love to make with my Cricut machines.

If I didn't know any better, I would think these Woven Baskets are the real deal!
Photo via: Designs by Mandee

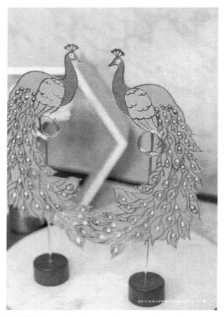

You wouldn't think these Die Cut Peacocks are made out of paper, would you?
Photo via: Designs by Mandee

CRICUT 101: EVERYTHING YOU NEED TO KNOW ABOUT CRIC... | 29

I'm a Potterhead, and if you're one too, you will love how many awesome Harry Potter-theme projects you can make with a Cricut machine! Photo via: Designs by Mandee

These are just some of the things you can do with a Cricut. But, there's more. A lot more! Let's take a look at what else you can do with Cricut machines.

Greeting Cards

With a Cricut machine, you can create pop-out cards, cut-out cards, and even 3D cards that will really make someone's day.

Besides using the cutting tool in your Cricut machine, you can also use the writing tool to write on the cards with laser-like precision using many fonts. Not only your cards are pretty, but they'll also have your personal touch.

These are just some of the type of greeting cards you can make with a Cricut machine.

14 - Dazzle your loved ones with all kinds of cutout greeting cards Photo via: Cricut Inspiration

15 - Sleek and sophisticated thank you card that will mean so much Photo via: Anastasia Anastasia

16 - Mark special occasions with beautiful cards you can make yourself Photo via: Cricut

CRICUT 101: EVERYTHING YOU NEED TO KNOW ABOUT CRIC... | 31

Decals

You can practically use decals for anything and everything around the house, from making labels in your kitchen to personalizing your gadgets to decorating your home with tasteful designs.

Between decals and stickers, I much prefer decals for my art projects. Decals last longer, and it gives a better finish when applied. You will usually need heat or water to ensure maximum adhesion.

Decals are thicker than your average peel-and-stick sticker labels, but you don't have to worry about making accurate cuts when you have a Cricut machine.

To give you an idea of what you can do with decals, take a look at some of these.

17 - Label your jars with decals to give them a sophisticated or whimsical look
Photo via: Cricut

18 - Label things with beautiful and cute designs using decals Photo via: Cricut

What I love about decals is there's practically nothing you can't use it for. Another favorite of mine is to decorate my wall with decals. It adds a splash of accent to your living space and also brightens up any room. You can get many ideas online or download and cut designs from Cricut design software.

Cardstock décor

I usually go crazy with cardstock décor when it's time for Halloween or Christmas.

I love cardstock for its beautiful and vibrant colors and because it's a comfortable material to work with. It's much thicker and more durable than the average paper, but it's still very flexible to be shaped into almost anything you can imagine. Cardstock is also great for kids' projects since children are very creative when it comes to making colorful things. You can use cardstock on your Cricut machine to help cut fun shapes for your kids' art projects and see what they can come up with!

With cardstock décor, I'm not just talking about Christmas or Halloween decors. You can make any design or shape for practically any occasion. I've used my Cricut machine to make cardstock décor for birthdays, anniversaries, baby showers, graduations; you name it.

To make cardstock décor with a Cricut machine, decide on the designs you want. I find it helpful to browse online, looking for inspiration. Even though some designs I found are made from other materials, you can replicate them just the same with a Cricut machine using cardstock.

Let's take a look at some of my favorite things to make when it comes to cardstock décor.

20 - Make fun and cute streamers for birthday parties Photo via: Cricut

21 - Get creative and make Halloween decorations using cardstock Photo via: June Gathercole

CRICUT 101: EVERYTHING YOU NEED TO KNOW ABOUT CRIC... | 33

23 - Use cardstock to make novel pieces of contemporary art Photo via: Mel Poole

Scrapbooking stickers and décors

From personalizing your scrapbook pages or creating your very own stickers and decals, the Cricut machine is a gift to all scrapbookers.

Whether you're looking to cut specific personal designs for your scrapbook stickers, or you want to add a touch of foil to your cardstock paper, you can use the Cricut machine for these.

If you're a scrapbooker and looking for ideas, here's what you can do with a Cricut machine. You can cut stickers, cardstock, ribbons, fabrics, decals, and many other materials into any design or shape you want.

24 - Add texture, colors, and shapes to your scrapbook page with fun motifs Photo via: Designs by Miss Mandee

25 - Design and cut your own scrapbooking stickers with a Cricut Photo via: Pure Julia

Iron-on Vinyl

I'm crazy about iron-on vinyl too. It's a terrific material to use, especially in your fabric projects, because they can turn a boring t-shirt into something quirky in an instant. You can use iron-on vinyl to add a personal touch to your clothing or home items. I love iron-on vinyl on cushion covers because it can light up my couch just like that.

Another great thing about iron-on vinyl is that it's not expensive at all! doesn't cost a bomb! Iron-on vinyl is not expensive, and you can find them at the dollar store or a gift shop. This material is easy to handle and even easier to apply. Just make sure you read the instructions carefully about working with vinyl since it takes several steps before you can finally transfer the design onto your items.

There are many things you can do with iron-on vinyl. For example, you can give your old clothing a facelift or use it to place a monogram on totes or purses to give it a classy and sophisticated look. Just a small gold iron-on vinyl at the corner of your jacket or cardigan can change your outfit from drab to fab. You can also add stylish monograms to your sneakers, phone casings, or backpacks.

Here are some of my favorite designs for iron-on vinyl.

CRICUT 101: EVERYTHING YOU NEED TO KNOW ABOUT CRIC... | 35

27 - I don't know about you, but I just love quirky t-shirts Photo via: Sincerely Media

28 - Add iron-on vinyl on cushion covers to give your home a little flavor Photo via: Maxim Lugovnin

Stamps

Here's another fun project that I think you will love to explore. Making stamps from foam, corkboard, or rubber sheet is something I thoroughly enjoy creating. These stamps really make your items or greeting cards unique. You can turn anything chic and handmade with one of these stamps.

I usually love using stamps on my greeting cards and also on my kitchen towels. Using some acrylic paint, I will stamp design on my kitchen towels, so not only my towels are customized, but it also adds a spark of colors and life into my kitchen.

Here are some stamp designs you can cut with a Cricut machine.

30 - Personalized your swaddle blanket with your very own stamps Photo via: Designs by Miss Mandee

So, there you have it.

As you can see, there's nothing you can't create with a Cricut machine. These are just some of the project ideas I love to do with my Cricut machine, and I'm sure there are many more things you can create once you get the hang of using the machine.

And to excite you even more, I'm sharing a lot more project ideas as well as the step-by-step guide on how to create these projects in my third book, *"Cricut Project and Profit Ideas for 2021 and Beyond: The Beginner's Step-by-Step Guide to Tons of Project Ideas and Making Money Fast with Cricut"*.

If you love the possibility of creating awesome projects, then you definitely shouldn't miss the third book of this series!

Now that you've discovered a taste of what you can create with a Cricut machine, I'm sure you're excited to know more about it so you can fully maximize its usage.

In the next chapter, I'll walk you through the tools and accessories of a Cricut machine. Before you begin your crafting endeavors with this fantastic machine, it's essential to know the tools you will need and use in your craft projects.

2

ALL YOU NEED TO KNOW ABOUT CRICUT TOOLS AND ACCESSORIES

Now that you know what you can do with a Cricut machine let's take a more in-depth look at this machine's inner workings.

So, in this chapter, we'll take a closer look at the tools that come with a Cricut machine.

Not only tools can help you craft better, but it's also handy when it comes to customizing your machine to your needs. Other than that, understanding the way your machine works is also a great way to identify an issue should anything happen.

Let's dive right into a Cricut machine to know more about this wonderful piece of equipment.

BLADES & TOOLS AND THEIR FUNCTIONS

The blades of a Cricut machine is what sets this machine from many other die-cutters.

I'm not only talking about its quality, which is top-notch, but also the versatility and capabilities. Whether you're looking to cut, score, deboss, engrave, or perforate, Cricut machine blades are carefully designed so you can achieve commercial-grade projects every time.

Before we begin, a word of caution:

All Cricut machine blades are incredibly sharp. Please be extra careful and mindful when handling them, especially during swapping.

And now, let's first take a look at the Cricut blades.

All-Purpose Blade

34 - Photo via: Cricut

This is the most basic blade that you'll use with your Cricut Joy. Even though this blade is not compatible with other advanced Cricut models, the All-Purpose Blade is a mighty tool. Its primary function is to perform any form of regular DIY cutting. It may seem like a simple blade, but you can confidently use the All-Purpose Blade to cut many different materials that your Cricut Joy is compatible with.

The All-Purpose Blade is designed to resist wear and tear as well as strong against breakage. Hence, this is why this blade is compatible with more than 50+ materials. This means it can easily cut corrugated cardboard, poster board, cardstock, iron-on materials such as glitter mesh, holographic mosaic, infusible ink transfer sheets, HTV, leather, various types of paper, plastic as well as vinyl.

I have made Halloween lanterns, bridal shower streamers, and Christmas wreaths using the All-Purpose Blade on my Cricut Joy. I have also cut many HTV and infusible ink transfer sheets for my cushion covers and kids' t-shirts using the same blade. I mainly used cardstocks for most of the celebration projects, and I managed to achieve laser-precision cutouts for my decoration items.

When you purchase your Cricut Joy, the factory blade comes with housing. You can choose to buy additional blades as replacements. However, the blade and the housing are sold separately.

All-Purpose Blade

- Primary function: Perform all manner of cutting for everyday DIY projects
- Compatible materials: 50+ including HTVs, cardboards, cardstocks, plastic
- Model: Cricut Joy
- Available at: Cricut, Amazon

Premium Fine-Point Blade

35 - Photo via: Cricut

As the name suggests, this fine blade is specifically designed to perform delicate cuts of even the most intricate designs. This blade can cut thin to medium-weight materials with ease, so you don't have to worry about tear risks. It's made from German carbide steel of premium quality, and despite its delicate function, the Premium Fine-Point Blade is tough and resistant to wear and tear.

If you're a designer or crafter who works with thin or delicate materials, I'm sure you'll love the Premium Fine-Point Blade. While the blade may not look like a dainty item, I can assure you it works like magic. This blade can smoothly perform intricate cuts on faux leather, notebook paper, washi sheet (one of my favorite materials!), pearl paper, and even parchment paper.

The blade is suitable for flower projects. I have used it on crepe paper to make elegant corsages and flower crowns. Since its fine blade can cut delicate and intricate designs, you can also use it to make lace design greeting cards. The cut is extremely precise that all it took was a gentle tap to remove the cutouts' negative portions.

Previously, this blade was known as the Premium German Carbide blade. The new and improved Premium Fine-Point Blade is strengthened to resist breakage and made to last much longer even with many hours of cutting. However, the sharpness of the blade does depend on how often you use it.

Premium Fine-Point Blade

- Primary function: Perform intricate cutting on delicate materials
- Compatible materials: Paper, vinyl, iron-on, adhesive foil, aluminum foil, construction paper, cork sheet, faux suede, glitter vinyl, washi tape, wax paper
- Model: Cricut Maker, Cricut Explore Air™ 2, Cricut Explore Air™, Cricut Explore One
- Available at: Cricut, Amazon

Deep-Point Blade

36 - Photo via: Cricut

Cricut understands and knows that there are times you need to perform intricate cuts on thicker or tougher materials. It's not uncommon for crafters or designers who don't have efficient tools to avoid making intricate designs on rigid materials. This is why the Deep-Point Blade is such a brilliant solution! This blade is part of Cricut's fine point blade series, so you know it can perform the most intricate cuts.

I've tried cutting lace designs on materials such as craft foam, metallic leather, and aluminum foil. The key to why the Deep-Point Blade can perform intricate cuts on tougher materials is its steeper blade angle. Compared to the Premium Fine-Point Blade, this blade is made from more durable steel. The blade's material and its angle both work great to give you ornate finishings on sturdier materials.

I find this blade to be the best blade to use when cutting craft foam. There were many occasions where I cut colorful craft foam for my kids' art project as well as pieces for festive decorations. Typically, if you use scissors to cut craft foam, the sheet doesn't hold its shape and may bend, so you end up with jagged edges. But the Deep-Point Blade provides such precise and accurate cuts for craft foam that I don't think I'll ever use scissors again!

The Deep-Point Blade is suitable for a wider variety of materials, and you can cut materials of up to 1.5mm in thickness.

Deep-Point Blade

- Primary function: Perform intricate cutting on thicker materials
- Compatible materials: Stiffened felt, magnet, chipboard, foam sheets, thick cardstock, stamp material, genuine leather, natural wood veneer
- Model: Cricut Maker, Cricut Explore Air™ 2, Cricut Explore Air™, Cricut Explore One
- Available at: Cricut, Amazon

Bonded-Fabric Blade

37 - Photo via: Cricut

I think you'll understand that one of the biggest crafters' pet peeves is when someone accidentally uses your fabric scissors to cut other materials. For crafters who are particular about which scissors they use when cutting specific material, Cricut offers you a specially made Bonded-Fabric Blade. This premium blade is made to cut bonded fabric and many types of fabric.

As much as all Cricut blades are sharp and can last a long time, you can have one blade that should only be used for cutting fabric. The Bonded-Fabric Blade is pink in color to match its FabricGrip mat. The color helps you tell right away which blade you're using, so don't make the mistake of using the wrong blade for the wrong kind of material.

I cut burlap and denim when I make my makeup pouch and my kids' pencil cases. I'm also a fan of handmade headbands and quilt blankets, so I've cut cotton and lace for these projects too.

Do note that you can still cut fabric with other Cricut blades. However, using the specially made Fabric-Bonded Blade is better because the blade provides clean and accurate cuts even on thin fabric. Cutting fabric with other Cricut blades may cause drag on the material and cause your fabric to fray or even tear. Not only that, using the right blade for the right kind of material helps to prolong the life of the blade.

Fabric-Bonded Blade

- Primary function: Perform cuts on fabric
- Compatible materials: Oilcloth, polyester, bonded silk
- Model: Cricut Maker, Cricut Explore Air™ 2, Cricut Explore Air™, Cricut Explore One
- Available at: Cricut, Amazon

Rotary Blade

38 - *Photo via: Cricut*

The Rotary Blade is an excellent blade that you can use for almost any imaginable project. Whether you need to cut burnout velvet or canvas or even Chantilly lace, the Rotary Blade does the job for you, and it does it damn well. Made from premium stainless steel, this Rotary Blade has 10 times the cutting power compared to other Cricut blades.

Since the Rotary Blade is made for customizable projects that require precise cuttings, this blade is often used for home sewing. However, you can still use it on many other types of materials to perform standard, detailed, or free form designs. Some of the materials that can be cut with the Rotary Blade are charmeuse satin, crepe paper, faux suede, tissue paper, and oilcloth.

If you're a designer who works most often with fabric or bonded fabric, I know you'll love the Rotary Blade. There are endless projects you can create using the Rotary Blade. Whether you need to make fabric appliques for your kids' backpack or cutting up delicate lace for accents on a dress, you can use the Rotary Blade to make precise cuts. You don't have to be a tailor to work with the Rotary Blade. I've used the blade to cut fabric for pillowcases, totes, aprons, baby and doll clothes, and even stuffed animals!

It can be challenging to cut free form edges on delicate fabrics, so this is why you need to use the FabricGrip mat when using the Rotary Blade to cut fabric. This mat gives a better and more secure hold on your fine material. Do note that the Rotary Blade will work exclusively on Cricut Maker because it's made for both pro-level and heavy-duty cutting.

Rotary Blade

- Primary function: Perform cuts on fabric and customized/free form designs
- Compatible materials: Organza, tulle, nylon, mulberry paper, linen, kevlar, wool, felt, acrylic fabric, extra heavy fabric, cotton
- Model: Cricut Maker
- Available at: Cricut, Amazon

Knife Blade

39 - Photo via: Cricut

I would like you to meet the Chuck Norris of Cricut Blades. It's made to withstand thick and tough materials. The extra-deep knife can slice through dense materials with ease. Not only that, but it's also highly durable and safe, so you can use it without any worry. Since this blade is made for heavy-duty cutting of thick materials, it's recommended that you use it to cut moderate detail designs. The cutting pressure on this blade is immense, so you shouldn't cut designs that are smaller than ¾ inches, including the size of the interior cut. The blade's pressure will cause your material to fall apart or separate if your designs are too small or intricate.

The Knife Blade is stable and resilient. When I say that it can cut through thick materials, I really mean thick ones. You can easily cut illustration boards or garment leather. This makes the Knife Blade a great tool for designers who make models and miniatures. Despite the thick material often used in this type of projects, the Knife Blade provides accurate and precise cuts. I don't work with thick boards that much, but I've tried cutting chipboards before, and it turned out perfect.

I've seen some of my miniaturist friends who make such fantastic items using the Knife Blade. Even though the materials they use were thick and dense, I was impressed with how they can make precise cuts with the Knife Blade. Not only that, but I've also seen some interior designers who make exquisite 3D models. Some other projects you can make with the Knife Blade include chipboard gift tags, dollhouses, and wooden doorplates.

To give you the exact cut you're looking for, the Knife Blade will make several shallow initial cuts on the material. With each repetition, the machine will add gradual pressure on the blade to make better and deeper cuts. Besides ensuring proper and precise cuts on your dense materials, this technique also provides your machine is not overexerted.

Knife Blade

- Primary function: Perform heavy-duty cuts on dense & thick materials
- Compatible materials: Balsa wood, basswood, damask chipboard, matboard, tooling leather, heavy chipboard
- Model: Cricut Maker
- Available at: Cricut, Amazon

The following tools are additional Machine Tools that you can have with your Cricut machine. Most of these tools are only compatible with a Cricut Maker because the tools' functions are more suited for pro-level designers.

Let's take a look at some of the other cool and unique additional Machine Tools Cricut offers.

Scoring Wheel & Double Scoring Wheel

40 - Photo via: Cricut

The Scoring Wheel and the Double Scoring Wheel are parts of Cricut's QuickSwap Tools set. In terms of scoring tools, Cricut makes two types of scoring tools. One is a Scoring Wheel and Double Scoring Wheel, and the other one is the Scoring Stylus. We'll talk about the latter in a moment.

Cricut Scoring Wheel comes in two models, a single wheel and a double wheel. This nifty little tool is a great one to use when you need to score any of your project material. The scoring tool can be used for many functions.

The Single Scoring Wheel is perfect for making creases or score lines on thin- to medium-weight materials such as cardstock or cardboard. On the other hand, the Double Scoring Wheel can create two parallel lines that are deep enough for heavier materials such as poster boards or art illustration boards. Since these materials are thick, you need two score lines to have a seamless fold.

Before I had a Cricut machine, I made creases on my greeting cards and envelopes using a ruler. While it does the job, the ruler's edges sometimes hurt my material and sometimes even left tear marks. With the Scoring Wheel, you can make precise and perfect creases without compromising your material's quality and condition. The Scoring Wheel has ten times more pressure than the Scoring Stylus, giving you sharp and neat crease folds.

You can use both the Scoring Wheel and Double Scoring Wheel on a number of materials. Other than cardstock and cardboard, I've also used the Scoring Wheel on an art illustration board, foil paper, and kraft board. Just like the Knife Blade, the Scoring Wheel also applies gradual pressure on your materials, so you'll get that sharp and precise crease every time. With the Scoring Wheel, you can get foldable artwork effortlessly because the deep score lines will make folding and creasing easy breezy for you.

There are many things you can use the Scoring Wheel for. As mentioned, I use it to make precise crease fold for my greeting cards and envelopes. You can also use the scoring wheel to make 3D home décors or 3D models, or you can even score designs on a board for your kids' dollhouse.

Scoring Wheel & Double Scoring Wheel

- Primary function: Perform score lines and scoring designs
- Compatible materials: Cereal box, cork, corrugated cardboard, crepe paper, heavy cardstock, light chipboard, pearl paper, photo paper, vellum
- Model: Cricut Maker
- Available at: Cricut, Amazon

The following four tools are a part of Cricut's QuickSwap Tools set. This set is only compatible with a Cricut Maker because their functions suit pro-level and advanced crafting projects. All tools in this set use QuickSwap housing. The QuickSwap housing is a devilishly simple way to swap your tools at a click of a button. The tools in the QuickSwap Tools all work perfectly with one housing that works for all.

Debossing Tip

42 - Photo via: Cricut

You can add a touch of elegance and sophistication to your projects with one amazing tool. The Debossing Tip is one of Cricut's ever-expanding suite of tools, and it's perfect when you need to add debossing texture or feature to your materials. This tip can create beautiful deboss patterns, including monograms or seals.

At times, you may not want to cut out on your materials because you want to go with something more subtle and soft. The Debossing Tip works well on many types of materials. While you can also use the Scoring Wheels to deboss, I find that the Debossing Tip is the perfect tool for the job because it creates finer and more delicate patterns.

With just a few tasteful debossing details on your materials, you can truly transform how your projects look. You can add a lot of depth to your project with the Debossing Tip. I used the Debossing Tip to make graceful and dainty lace patterns on my wedding invitation card orders for many occasions. As for my personal use, I have used the tip to deboss faux leather that I use to make elegant and unique hair berets.

Another interesting note, if you're curious about whether the Debossing Tip can create an embossed look or not, I must say that I've tried this before, and the result wasn't that great. I was using cardstock to test this effect, so perhaps if you were to use a thinner paper, maybe the result will differ.

Debossing Tip

- Primary function: Perform deboss patterns and lines
- Compatible materials: Construction paper, duct tape sheet, foil poster board, glitter cardstock, kraft board, pearl paper, tooling leather
- Model: Cricut Maker
- Available at: Cricut, Amazon

Engraving Tip

43 - Photo via: Cricut

This is another fantastic tool in the QuickSwap Tools. The Engraving Tip creates permanent designs onto your material so you can add more texture, depth, and accent to your projects. This tip is made to perform professional-looking engraving on many types of materials.

The Engraving Tip has a strong tip made from premium carbide steel, allowing precise and sharp engraving on your materials. You can create beautiful designs on anodized aluminum, kraft board, or poster board. However, it's essential to make sure the type of materials you use is suitable for the Engraving Tip. Even though the tip is sharp enough to engrave thick materials, prolonged use on unsuitable materials can damage your tool.

You can make lovely dog tags for your pets. Engraving is also an excellent way to make keepsakes or mementos because you can engrave inspirational quotes or important dates on wood veneer or leather. Many people like to receive personalized gifts, so engraving special symbols or words that mean something to them on a beautiful material is a lovely way to express how you feel.

When using your Engraving Tip, don't be alarmed if your tip lifts and spins for several seconds. This is an automated process to ensure longer use on your tip and mitigate wear and tear on your tool.

Engraving Tip

- Primary function: Perform engraving
- Compatible materials: Acetate, faux leather, genuine leather, heavy watercolor paper, metallic leather, vinyl record
- Model: Cricut Maker
- Available at: Cricut, Amazon

Perforation Blade

44 - Photo via: Cricut

There's something immensely satisfying when you can cleanly tear away a piece of paper from its perforation line. A sharp perforation line is always desirable for many crafters. Whether we use it to make a homemade journal or a ticket booklet for our kids' school concert, making perforation is always fun.

Many of us have used the manual or handheld perforation tool before, and I think we would all agree how it doesn't always give the result we want. It requires one to have a steady hand while at the same time applying the same amount of pressure to ensure deep enough perforation. On the other hand, the Cricut Perforation Blade is a tool that will make your perforation task much easier and faster. It cuts clean and evenly spaced perforation on your materials so you can create many creative projects.

I love the Perforation Blade because it can make clean and sharp perforations on many different types of material. With Cricut's Perforation Blade, I've cut a wide range of everyday craft materials such as cardstock, construction paper, craft foam, and crepe paper. You too can make many fun projects with the Perforation Blade, such as homemade scrapbook paper, raffle tickets for scrapbook decors, or tear-away notepad on your fridge.

I don't have any complaints about the Perforation Blade except that you cannot customize the perforation gaps. In some perforation tools, you can swap the perforation wheel to customize the gaps' size, where you can choose a wide gap or a closer one. As for the Cricut Perforation Blade, this tool has 2.5mm teeth that create 0.5mm gaps.

Perforation Blade

- Primary function: Perform clean and sharp perforation
- Compatible materials: Acetate, heavy crepe paper, felt, foil acetate, glitter cardstock, kraft cardstock and board, metallic poster board, parchment paper, photo paper, tooling leather, washi sheet
- Model: Cricut Maker
- Available at: Cricut, Amazon

Wavy Blade

45 - Photo via: Cricut

With the Wavy Blade, you can cut wavy lines without any hassle or worry.

Among the materials I have used with the Wavy Blade are felt, construction paper, copy paper, and craft foam. As you can probably tell by now, these are the most common items I use in my crafting. However, I know and have seen the wavy blade used on other materials such as crepe paper. The Wavy Blade makes such precise cuts that you can use it on something as thin as fine crepe paper. Not only that, but you can use the Wavy Blade on fabric, and it still gives you the same accurate and precise cutting as it does on paper.

I've made party flag cake toppers from washi paper using this tool, and I've also made many gift tags. I've also cut decal and sticker labels with the Wavy Blade, and there was no issue at all where the lines weren't cut properly. The precise and even wavy lines really give my decoration items a clean and professional look.

You can rely on the Wavy Blade to create whimsical and free form wavy lines in half the time it takes to use pinking shears or a drag blade. However, remember that just like the Knife Blade, the Wavy Blade is really sharp. So, be careful when handling it.

Wavy Blade

- Primary function: Perform clean and sharp wavy lines
- Compatible materials: Everyday iron-on, stiff felt, flannel, cotton, fleece, embossed paper, fusible fabric, heavy cardstock, holographic sparkle mosaic, HTV, linen, polyester, vinyl, tooling leather
- Model: Cricut Maker
- Available at: Cricut, Amazon

These are additional tools you can use with several Cricut machine models.

Foil Transfer Tool

46 - *Photo via: Cricut*

This is the latest tool in Cricut's arsenal, and I'm absolutely in love with it. Introduced in September 2020, the Foil Transfer tool just makes everything about your project better and, oh, so much prettier! Unlike other foil transfer tools in the market, the Cricut's Foil Transfer Tool doesn't require any heat to perform foil transfer. Instead, it uses a special pressure system to activate the foil and evenly transfer it to your materials.

Basically, you can use the Foil Transfer Tool to transfer foil onto any kind of material. As long as the material is smooth, your foil will transfer evenly. The smoother the material, the better is the transfer. You can transfer foil onto materials such as cardstock, and for me, this gives the best effect I'm looking for when it comes to foil transfer. Other compatible materials include heavy watercolor paper, copy paper, and photo paper.

With the Foil Transfer Tool, you can add some sparkle and shine to almost anything! Whether you're decorating a greeting card or adding some dimensions to the corners of your scrapbook pages, the Foil Transfer Tool can foil your project within seconds. Since this tool can transfer the foil of any design, you can let your imagination run wild. You can create beautiful shiny mandalas on a mounting board, or you can decorate your leather wristband with ethnic or contemporary designs.

The sheet you need to use with the Foil Transfer Tool can be of various types. Whether you use a heat-activated sheet or not, the Foil Transfer Tool can transfer foil onto your materials. However, for best results, I strongly recommend you use Cricut Foil Transfer. The transfer sheet comes in various colors where you need to tape it over your base material to foil your design. The Foil Transfer tool also has three different tip sizes, i.e., fine, medium, and bold. You can easily swap between tips for the same design or project.

However, please note that the Cricut Foil Transfer Tool may not effectively transfer all foil onto your base material. For obvious reasons, the Cricut Foil Transfer sheet works best. But other brands such as Spellbinders Glimmer Hot Foil or WRMK Heat Activated Foil can work with this tool even though these brands are heat-activated foils. You may trial and error on other foil transfer sheet brands to see which can get the job done, but based on my experience, heat-activated foil may not be as shiny as Cricut's own Foil Transfer Sheet.

Foil Transfer Tool

- Primary function: Perform foil transfer on various materials
- Compatible materials: Deluxe paper, pearl paper, vellum, kraft board, faux leather
- Model: Cricut Maker, Cricut Explore Air™ 2, Cricut Explore Air™
- Available at: Cricut, Amazon

PENS & MARKERS

Just like many crafters out there, I'm a sucker for stationery. So, you can imagine how excited I am with the Cricut Pen range. With over 70 different types of pens to choose from, it's a wonder how I still manage to control myself at times!

While I do own craft pens from many different brands, what I like about Cricut pens is their distinct quality. The color quality of Cricut pens, to me, is one of the best in the market. It writes smoothly, and the ink consistency gives you an even finish in any of your handwriting works. As for the machine pens, it also writes smoothly and accurately since the tips are highly well-made. Not only that, I notice Cricut pens and markers tend to lose their ink only after prolonged use compared to other brands' arts and crafts pens.

Cricut pens range has two categories where one type can be used for Cricut machines, and the other category is Infusible Ink™ freehand markers. The great thing is that you can use pens and markers on all Cricut models!I love Cricut pens and markers because all Cricut machines can use a pen for its writing and drawing purposes. And their Infusible Ink™ freehand markers can be used with EasyPress™ machines, so they turn permanent on your project's surface.

Since the Cricut pens and markers range is quite extensive, I'll break this section into several sections. I believe these sections will help you understand the uses and functions of these Cricut pens and markers better. This way, you won't have to guess or worry if you're using the right pen for the right task.

Which Cricut machine uses Cricut pens?

Guess what? In case you've forgotten, all Cricut machines use Cricut pens! From Cricut Joy to Cricut Maker, you have an array of choices for the types of pens you can use. However, with the exception of Cricut Joy, all other pens and markers can be used interchangeably between the machines. Cricut Joy, because of its smaller and compact size, has smaller pens.

47 - Cricut Joy is an excellent companion for crafters who enjoy typography Photo via: Cricut

The Cricut pens and markers are truly amazing. All you have to do is place them in the clamp holder in your machine and you're good to go. There are dual clamp holders for models such as Explore Air™ 2 and Maker. These dual holders allow you to multitask with the Write-then-Cut or Draw-then-Cut setting. In Cricut Joy, however, you have to swap between your pens and your blades.

ALL YOU NEED TO KNOW ABOUT CRICUT TOOLS AND ACCES... | 51

With the Cricut pens and markers, you can have beautiful writings on your projects. The design software for Cricut machines has many free typography designs and fonts you can choose from. If you want more options or something more personalized, you can also load your own font into your design software. The font installation is super easy because it works the same way as to how you'd install font to your Photoshop or FontBook.

Getting to know your Cricut pens

When it comes to Cricut pens and markers, you are spoiled for choice. From Fine Point to Extra Fine Point to Gel Pens to Washable Fabric Pen, you can choose from any of these to make your projects stand out. Cricut pens are usually in a pack of five, but you can also find the Ultimate Sets, where it's a box of 30.

Except for the Cricut Joy pens, because it's smaller, all Cricut pens have subtle differences in their barrels and end caps. Since it's very common for crafters to store their pens upside down for more extended usage, Cricut cleverly indicates their pens at the bottom with the tip size. You can see pens marked with F, XF, M, GG, etc., so it's easy for you to reach for the right one within seconds.

Now, let's take a look at the Cricut pen range that you can use with your machine.

Fine Point Pens (F)

48 - Photo via: Cricut

With 30 different colors to choose from, you can create an everlasting impression on your projects. Whether you want to draw on it or write inspirational quotes or send intimate messages, you can count on the Fine Point Pens set to express what you feel and think.

This Fine Point Pens set is the most basic pens you should get for your Cricut machine. You can use it to write on almost anything, and you will get stunning results every time.

There are several Fine Point Pens sets, but I love the Ultimate Fine Point Pens set the most because it has a wide range of various bright and vibrant colors. With a fine 0.4mm tip, this Fine Point Pens set can write or draw the most detailed and fine design or words on your materials.

Other Fine Point Pens sets include the Wisteria, Tapestry, Martha Stewart Lily Pond, and Sherbet. There are also separate Fine Point Pens set for Cricut Joy. You will still get the same dynamic color range, but Cricut Joy pens are only different in size. All these sets can help you create a vibrant versatility in your projects.

Extra Fine Point Pens (XF)

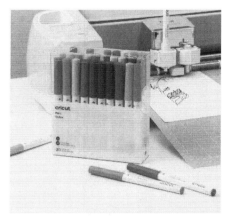

49 - Photo via: Cricut

Cricut's Extra Fine Point Pens set is one of the best fine point pens I've used. The tip is 0.3mm, they're suitable for your Cricut machine, and you can also use them to draw by hand. With 30 different colors, you can't go wrong with the Extra Fine Point Pens for all your embellishment work, papercrafts, or decorating greeting cards with small details.

Even though there aren't many colors available, you'll still love the color variety in the Extra Fine Point Pens sets. Compared to the Ultimate Fine Point Pens set, I personally prefer the range of colors in the Ultimate Extra Fine Point Pens set because they're brighter. I think you too will love colors like Very Berry, Candy Crystal, and Sour Apple.

Infusible Ink™ Markers (M)

Watch how your designs transfer from your computer to your machine to your projects. With these incredibly versatile markers, you can see your design blooms into pro-quality transfers with a heat press. Cricut Infusible Ink™ markers are medium point (1.0mm) and water-based, but they won't flake, fade, crack, or peel once dried.

If you like working with heat transfer materials like me, you'll surely enjoy and love Cricut's Infusible Ink™ markers. Once the ink comes in contact with a heat press, the ink will fuse with your materials, creating permanent and long-lasting wear. The bright colors of the Infusible Ink™ markers make your design stand out against any items such as tote bags, handkerchiefs, or t-shirts.

50 - Photo via: Cricut

The tip of Cricut's Infusible Ink™ markers is quite thick, so that these markers won't be suitable for fine or intricate designs/wordings. To use these markers, you need to have compatible Infusible Ink™ blanks, and the heat press you use needs to reach 400°F (205°).

Gel Pens (G)

51 - Photo via: Cricut

Gel pens are sophisticated, don't you think? They provide such a glossy or silky finish that everything you write on looks fancy and luxurious. What makes gel pens write smoothly is the rollerball in their nip instead of a felt tip. I love how gel pen glides smoothly over materials and produces such stunning effects.

Cricut's Gel Pens come in 0.8mm size, and the range has such bold colors. Compatible with models before Cricut Joy, the gel pens can help you create beautiful designs on your papercrafts. I admit some crafters are not highly artistic when it comes to handwritten designs or wordings. So, using the Cricut for writing and drawing tasks with the right pen is truly an advantage.

There are several color ranges in Cricut Gel Pen. To be honest, I don't have a favorite color range when it comes to the Gel Pens because every one of them is great to use. For example, the Fingerpaint range has bright and bold colors such as red, yellow, blue, and orange that are great for children's birthday party invitation cards. And for something that's more spunky, I usually use the Milky Gel Pen Set in Urban Rainbow. This set of pink, blue, orange, mint, and yellow gives me an edgy and modern look to my papercraft.

Like other Cricut pens and markers, the Gel Pens set is also water-based, non-toxic, and acid-free.

These are the types of amazingly wonderful arts and crafts pens and markers that Cricut carries.

Now let's take a look at the table below for a quick comparison of the pens and markers. I've categorized them according to their main types, i.e., Ultimate Sets, Pen Sets, Infusible Ink™ Markers, and Infusible Ink™ Freehand Markers. The pens and markers in the table below are compatible with Cricut Maker, Cricut Explore Air™ 2, and Cricut Explore Air™

Ultimate Sets

Fine Point (0.4mm)	30 colors
Extra Fine Point (0.3mm)	30 colors
Gel Pens	30 colors
Infusible Ink™ Markers	30 colors

Pen Sets

Fine Point (0.4mm) 5 colors / set	Tapestry Wisteria Sorbet Martha Stewart Slate (3 ct) Martha Stewart Lily Pond Martha Stewart Bedford
Extra Fine Point (0.3mm) 5 colors / set	Bohemian Spring Rain Brights Gumball Martha Stewart Gilded Forest
Gel 5 colors / set	Metallic Dark Petals Peacock Milky Set Urban Rainbow Origins Fingerpaint Suburbia Disturbia
Glitter Gel 5 colors / set	Mermaid Brights Basics Fiesta Martha Stewart Classic
Everyday Collection 10 pens / set	3 medium-point gold pens (1.0mm) 3 medium-point silver pens (1.0.mm) 4 fine-point black pens (0.4mm)
Multi 5 pens / set	Gold Black Silver

Infusible Ink™ Markers

15 ct	Ultimate
5 ct	Water-color Splash Black Basics Neon Nostalgia

Infusible Ink™ Freehand Markers

2.0	Tropical
Dual-Tip	Tropical Basics
Brush Tip	Tropical Basics

As mentioned earlier, Cricut Joy has its own line of pens because of their smaller size. Here are the types of pens available for Cricut Joy and the color range. Please note that all Cricut Joy pens and markers only come in a set of 3.

Cricut Joy

Fine Point (0.4mm)	Black, Brown, Gray Red, Green, Violet
Extra Fine Point (0.3mm)	Blacks Red, Blue, Black
Gel Pens	Teal, Purple, Pink Black, Gray, Blue
Glitter Gel	Black, Gold, Silver Pink, Blue, Green
Infusible Ink™ Markers	Blacks Black, Red, Green Yellow, Blueberry, Tangerine Wild Aster, Bright Teal, Party Pink

Will non-Cricut pens work for my Cricut?

Technically, you can use any pen to perform writing or drawing with your Cricut machine, but you need to make sure they are the right size barrels. Since the Cricut pen holder clamp is designed to fit only Cricut pens, you will need an adapter to fit other brands' pens.

52 - You need to get this type of adapter before you can use other brands' pens on Cricut Photo via: Abbi Kirsten Collections

I have used Sharpie Art Pen, Sakura Gelly Roll, Pilot Precise, Crayola Supertips, Tombow Brush Pens, and Uni-ball Signo on my Cricut. All these pens require a pen adapter tool before you can use these pens on your Cricut. Once you have placed the adapter into your Cricut's pen holder, you can use the same functions to perform any writing or drawing tasks!

ART SUPPLIES & ACCESSORIES

Besides making awesome machines and great craft pens, Cricut also has many other supplies and accessories that you can choose from. And just like their machines and pens, you can expect the same high-quality and top-of-the-line products for Cricut's supplies and accessories.

So, in this final section, I will talk about some of the additional supplies and accessories you can find under Cricut.

Cricut Infusible Ink™

As I've shared with you earlier, I love working with heat transfer sheets because I enjoy making prints on cushion covers or t-shirts. One of the best materials to work with if you want to spice up your home decor items or give your clothing a facelift is the Infusible Ink™ Transfer Sheets.

But before we take a look at these transfer sheets, let's first understand what Infusible Ink™ from Cricut is.

Infusible Ink™ is a form of ink transfer that's heat activated. Compared to iron-on transfer or HTV (heat transfer vinyl), Infusible Ink™ is infused *into* the material when it comes in contact with heat. Instead of sticking to your base material's surface, such as a cushion cover or a blanket, the ink is transferred straight into the material, so it becomes permanent.

55 - Make your mark on plain t-shirts with the versatile Infusible Ink™ Photo via: Cricut

Many heat transfer materials are made to be permanent as well, but Infusible Ink™'s permanence gives a better and longer-lasting effect on your material. What I love about Infusible Ink™ is the final finishing on the material. Even though I prefer how HTV looks on my cushion covers, Infusible Ink™ will give your clothing a seamless look and weightless feel. If you were to run your hand over Infusible Ink™ designs, you wouldn't feel any bumps, outlines, or edges.

Many crafters use Infusible Ink™ on fabric such as t-shirts, gloves, shoes, or caps, but you can use Infusible Ink™ on other suitable materials as well. Express your creativity by applying the Infusible Ink™ on fun items such as coasters, makeup bags, or your baby's onesies!

There are two types of tools you can use to transfer Infusible Ink™ designs onto your materials.

One is using Infusible Ink™ pens, which you can place in your Cricut machine. We have covered Cricut pens and markers in earlier sections, so the Infusible Ink™ pens and markers work the same way as other Cricut pens.

When you have a design ready, you can place your Infusible Ink™ markers in your Cricut. Your machine will draw the design onto your heat transfer sheet and proceed to cut it so you can set the design on your base material. Once you have prepared your base material and placed the transfer sheet onto it, all you have to do is apply heat (hint: use your EasyPress™ 2 for the best result!), and voila!

56 - Draw any design with Cricut Infusible Ink™ markers Photo via: Sincerely Media

The second way to transfer a design onto your materials is to use the Infusible Ink™ Transfer Sheet. Now let's take a look at this second method.

Infusible Ink™ Transfer Sheets

A transfer sheet is the piece of material you place over your base material whenever you want to transfer a heat-activated design. You can either cut it into shapes to make whimsical or fancy design t-shirts. Or you can draw on it before cutting wordings out of it for beautiful and modern typography.

Cricut offers ready-cut transfer sheets under their Infusible Ink™ range. You can achieve a pro-level finish with these transfer sheets since they're made from high-quality material. Every Infusible Ink™ sheet is pre-inked and will release vibrant and bold colors or patterns when it comes in contact with a heat press. For maximum effect, your heat press needs to reach at least 385°F (196°C).

You can use Cricut pens to draw your designs on the sheet and cut it with your Cricut machine. For a better finish, use your EasyPress™ heat presses to transfer the design onto your materials. You can transfer the design from Cricut Infusible Ink™ Transfer Sheet onto materials such as ceramic coasters, pillowcases, t-shirts, or wine bags.

I love Cricut's transfer sheets because the transferred inks will never flake, peel, or crack, and I can attest to this.

Cricut Infusible Ink™ Transfer Sheets come in many different vibrant colors and fun pattern prints. You can create as many creative designs as you can think of.

The Rainbow Triangles Infusible Ink™ Transfer Sheet is one of my favorite patterns to use. It adds a whole lot of fun and colors to your t-shirts or beach bags that I think you won't be able to stop using it too!

57 - Give your t-shirts a fun facelift with the Watercolor Splash transfer sheets!
Photo via: Amazon

Other patterns include Rainbow Triangles, Leopard Print, Midnight Sky, and Mermaid Rainbow. The choices for solid colors are also awesome, where you can have Avocado, Bright Teal, Party Pink (my favorite shade!), Tangerine, and Ultra Violet.

Infusible Ink™ Transfer Sheets can be used for all Cricut models.

Cricut Mats

Using a die-cutting machine mat in your crafting projects is as important as the machine itself. Without the right mat, your material may slip or move, and this can ruin your projects.

Cricut makes sure that their mats are optimized for all your crafting materials and needs. Made with various grip strengths, all Cricut Mats provide the right hold on your materials, so you don't have to worry while cutting, writing, scoring, or drawing. Even though Cricut Mats give a firm grip on your materials, you'll be surprised with how easily you can remove your items after you're done!

Cricut Mats come in several categories where you need to use the right mat for the right kind of material and the appropriate purpose. Let's take a closer look at the Cricut Mats range so you know which one to use the next time you need to use it.

LightGrip Machine Mat (Blue)

59 - Photo via: Cricut

Specially engineered to hold a wide range of thin or lightweight materials, the LightGrip Mat is suitable for many common crafting materials.

This LightGrip Mat can provide a firm hold on your cardstock, standard paper, vellum, vinyl, or washi sheets. All Cricut Mats are slightly sticky, so your materials don't slip or move, but you don't have to worry about this. The adhesive on the mat will not tear or ruin your light material when you remove it from the surface.

There are two standard sizes for LightGrip Mats where 12" x 12" and the other are 12" x 24". The 12" x 12" mats are also sold in a set of 15 pieces. The LightGrip Machine Mat is compatible with the Cricut Maker and Cricut Explore line.

StandardGrip Machine Mat (Green)

60 - Photo via: Cricut

These are the most widely used mats made by Cricut. It usually comes together with your Cricut machine. I love the StandardGrip Machine Mat because it's versatile and can handle many common craft materials. The StandardGrip Mat is suitable for medium-weight materials such as cardstock, heat transfer vinyl, pattern papers, iron-on, and embossed cardstock.

Since this mat is used for many common craft materials, it's more carefully engineered to hold a wide range of medium-weight materials without any hassle.

There are two sizes for the StandardGrip Machine Mats. The 12" x 12" mats are sold in a set of 2 or 30 mats. The 12" x 24" mats are sold in a set of 2, 3, 0r 25 mats. These mats are compatible with Cricut Maker and Cricut Explore series.

StrongGrip Machine Mat (Purple)

61 - Photo via: Cricut

Cutting heavy, thick, or dense materials calls for the StrongGrip Machine Mat. This mat is carefully designed to provide a strong and firm grip on heavy materials.

It's crucial to make sure your heavy material is securely in place while you're cutting it. Among the reasons why your heavy materials need to be secure is to avoid any accidents, both on you or the machine. Improper fit or hold can damage your Cricut blades, and you also risk the material moving and causing you injury.

Many crafters who make models and miniatures use this mat. The StrongGrip Machine Mat is their trusty companion for cutting. Since they often work with heavy and thick materials such as poster boards, chipboard, and balsa wood, the StrongGrip Machine Mat gives them total hold and security.

StrongGrip Machine Mats are sold at 1 piece per pack and in two standard sizes of 12" x 12" and 12" x 24". This mat is compatible with Cricut Maker and Cricut Explore machines.

FabricGrip Machine Mat (Pink)

62 - Photo via: Cricut

This is the latest machine mat released by Cricut. Compared to other mats, the FabricGrip Machine Mat is specifically designed and made to hold fabric during cutting. It's made with combined strength and high-density material so the FabricGrip Machine Mat can withstand increased pressure during cutting.

Since fabrics tend to be flimsy or very thin, you need a special mat to place your materials on to achieve accurate and precise cuts. For proper fabric cuts, make sure you use the correct blade to cut your materials: the Bonded-Fabric Blade or the Rotary Blade. The FabricGrip Machine Mat can cut any fabric, so have no worry if you need to cut denim, cotton, lace, felt, polyester, or canvas!

As with other Cricut machine mats, the FabricGrip Machine Mat comes in two standard sizes. The 12" x 12" mats are sold in a set of 2, while the 12" x 24" mats are sold in a set of 1 or 3 mats.

Cricut Joy Mat

63 - Photo via: Cricut

The Cricut Joy™ is so aptly named because it does bring joy to crafters who own them. Despite its small size, the Cricut Joy™ can still perform many incredible feats. And for these great feats, you need the right mats that are made especially for Cricut Joy™.

There are three types of Cricut Joy mats: LightGrip, StandardGrip, and Card Mat.

We have learned about the LightGrip and StandardGrip mats, so what is the Card Mat?

Since Cricut Joy™ is designed for simple DIY projects or quick last-minute tasks, the Card Mat (4.5" x 6.25") is used to hold your greeting cards or card inserts. While it'll work perfectly with all Cricut Joy™ cards, you can use the Card Mat to cut any greeting cards made from compatible materials. The Card Mat has standard greeting card measurements, so you can customize your cards smoothly.

Cricut Joy™ mats are sold in two sizes. The 4.5" x 12" size mats are available for StandardGrip and LightGrip, while the 4.5" x 6.5" is only available for the StandardGrip.

Self-Healing Mat

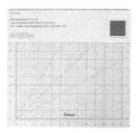

64 - Photo via: Cricut

Another great mat from Cricut is the Self-Healing Mat. Even though this mat is meant to be used in Cricut electronic cutting machines, it is a great companion for many crafters. As much as you can rely on your Cricut machine to perform any sort of cutting, there will be times when you want to cut your materials with a blade.

Other Cricut machine mats are sticky on one side to help grip your materials, but you can use both sides of the Self-Healing Mat. The mat is printed with easy-to-read and clear numbers with 1" border. It also has multi-angled grid lines to help you cut your materials better and accurately. What makes Cricut Self-Healing Mat better than its competitors is how this mat has 2 times more self-healing materials so that you will have a sturdier, stronger, and more longer lasting mat.

65 - Self-Healing Mat in Mint adds a little color and life to your work table Photo via: Cricut

The Self-Healing Mats come in three sizes: 12" x 12", 18" x 24", and 24" x 36". These mats also have three decorative prints (Mint, Rose, and Lilac), so you can choose the right one to brighten up your work table as you cut!

EasyPress Mat

66 - Photo via: Cricut

A high-quality heat press mat is vital when you're working with heat transfer materials. A poorly made mat can trap moisture, making your design moist and therefore risk flakiness, peeling off or fading. Not only that, a poorly made mat may also have poor insulation and can ruin your material and/or surface.

Cricut EasyPress Mats are made with special care and attention so your heat transfer projects will not be ruined. Its innovative construction can eliminate moisture as well as works well in directing heat to your iron-on designs. Furthermore, it also shields your work surface from any heat or moisture damage.

The EasyPress Mats have durable heat-resistant material and a foil layer that efficiently reflects heat to your iron-on designs for flawless transfers every time. Since we usually apply iron-on transfers on clothing, the EasyPress Mats also have a sponge layer in them. This sponge layer works both ways to insulate the work surface and a "pillow" to receive and absorb zippers and seams!

The mat comes in three different sizes: 8" x 10", 12" x 12", and 20"x 16". EasyPress mats are grey, but if you prefer something more spunky, you can get the 14" x 14" EasyPress Mats in Decorative Polka Dots. The Decorative Polka Dots line has two colors: Blue/Mint and Rose/Lilac.

67 - Add some spunk to your workspace with the Decorative Polka Dot EasyPress mat Photo via: Cricut

You should always use a mat that's either the same size as your press or a bigger one. Using a smaller mat than your EasyPress can prevent efficient and effective design transfer because you need even heat distribution for a successful transfer.

Cricut Machine Mats care

Here are some basic care techniques for your Cricut machine mats. These techniques can help maximize the performance of your mat and prolong its life. Plus, well-cared mats will provide smooth and accurate cuts for your projects.

68 - Cricut Scraper is a must-have Photo via: Amazon

- Clean your mat - Use your Cricut Scraper tool to remove any debris or particle on your mat. You should do this gently and methodically, preferably in one direction for

each scrape. Repeat this step until you're happy you've removed all debris on your mat. You can also clean your mat with warm soapy water and scrub it in a circular motion with a soft brush.
- Wipe down - Believe it or not, baby wipes are one of the most effective cleaning tools to clean mild build-up on your Cricut mat. However, make sure you use the gentle, alcohol-free baby wipes, or otherwise, your mat's adhesive material will be wiped off. A lint roller is also another good way to give your mat a wipe down, especially when the debris is too stubborn to remove with a scraper.
- Air dry - As much as it's tempting to quickly dry your mat with a towel or a kitchen towel, don't do this. The best way to dry your mat is to hang it to dry.
- Storing your mat - Your Cricut machine mats come with a protective film cover. Never throw this away. Use it to cover your Cricut mats whenever you're not using them.
- Right mat for the right materials - I can't stress enough how important this is. Different grip strengths on a mat mean different levels of adhesion. If you were to use light material on your StrongGrip mat, you'd have a hard time removing the material and thus causing more wear and tear on your purple mat. It's also important to be patient and take your time when removing your materials from your mat. Ripping it off or scraping it with your fingernails will only ruin your mat.

Cricut BrightPad

69 - Photo via: Cricut

Cricut BrightPad is a light-weight and low-profile light pad that helps to illuminate your projects so you can handle them in better lighting. The BrightPad helps to make crafting easier as it illuminates those fine lines that we need to see for tracing or cutting. This device has 5 different brightness settings so that you can adjust the lighting to your preference or need. The surface is made from premium quality material that's scratch-proof, to work on your projects on this light pad without worrying.

Plus, the BrightPad comes with a 6ft USB cord, so you don't have to worry that much about mobility. It's light-weight enough to carry it around, and it has a non-slip base, so it won't slip if you're using it on a drafting table.

Now we've taken an in-depth look at the Cricut machine models, the tools, and accessories, I would like to explore the materials you can use with a Cricut machine. As you know, Cricut machines are compatible with a wide range of materials. So, in the next chapter, I would like to share with you the types of materials you can use with your Cricut machine.

3

MATERIALS: WHAT CAN I CUT WITH MY CRICUT MAKER OR CRICUT EXPLORE SERIES?

There are numerous materials that you can cut, write, or score with any Cricut model. For this, Cricut takes great pride in the wide range of fabrics that their machines can cut. To know just how extensive their list of compatible materials is, let's take a look at the materials you can cut with the Cricut Explore series and the Cricut Maker.

Before we begin, I would like to highlight several important points:

- Do not use your Cricut machine to cut foodstuff such as fondant or nori as Cricut machines are not food-safe.
- Always handle all Cricut blades with care as the blades are made from premium steel and are very sharp.
- While there are many different materials listed below, Cricut doesn't guarantee the Cricut Explore and Cricut Maker can cut *all* materials.
- It's best to conduct a test cut on your unlisted material with similar material settings to see if you can achieve an accurate cut.
- Ensure the thickness of your material is not more than 2.0 mm when cutting with a Cricut Explore and not more than 2.4mm when using Cricut Maker.

Now that we got that out of the way, let's check out the materials you can cut!

CRICUT EXPLORE SERIES - COMPATIBLE MATERIALS

The Cricut Explore series can cut more than 100 materials. Here are some of the materials you can cut with the models in this series.

Material	Cut Pressure Setting	Blade Type
\multicolumn{3}{c}{Smart Set Dial Settings}		
Paper	153	
Paper +	162	
Vinyl	171	Fine-Point blade
Iron-on	185	
Light cardstock	272	Fine-Point blade
Cardstock	307	
Fabric	311	
Posterboard	333	

Smart Set Dial Settings — Predefined settings eliminate manual pressure, depth, and speed adjustment.

Custom Materials

For materials not listed in the Smart Set Dial setting above, move your knob to Custom and select your material from the dropdown list in Design Space

Adhesive foil	169	Fine-Point Blade
Aluminum – 0.14mm	327	
Aluminum foil	139	Deep-Point Blade
Birch	304	Fine-Point Blade
Burlap (Bonded)	344	Bonded Fabric Blade
Canvas	284	Fine-Point Blade
Cardstock (For intricate cuts)	219	
Chalkboard Vinyl	245	
Clear Printable Sticker Paper	240	
Construction Paper	163	
Cork, Adhesive-backed	135	
Corrugated Cardboard	312	Fine-Point Blade
Craft Foam	123	Deep-Point Blade

Denim, Bonded	321	Bonded Fabric Blade
Duct Tape Sheet	192	
Epoxy Glitter Paper	327	
Everyday Iron-On	185	
Everyday Iron-On Mosaic	280	
Faux Leather (Paper-thin)	300	Fine-Point Blade
Faux Suede	195	
Felt, Wool Bonded	331	
Flat Cardboard	306	
Foil Iron-On	165	
Glitter Iron-On	260	
Glitter Cardstock	327	
Grocery Bag	234	
Heavy Watercolor Paper	327	
Genuine Leather	270	Deep-Point Blade
Heavy Watercolor Paper	327	

Holographic Iron-On	240	
Holographic Iron-On Mosaic	310	Fine-Point Blade
Infusible Ink™ Transfer Sheet	260	
Laser Copy Paper	163	
Light Chipboard	327	Fine-Point blade
Light Glitter Paper	338	
Magnetic Sheet – 0.6mm	323	Deep-Point Blade
Medium Cardstock	299	Fine-Point Blade
Metallic Poster Board	299	
Natural Wood Veneer	345	Deep-Point Blade
Oil Cloth, Bonded	285	Bonded Fabric Blade
Pearl Paper	170	Fine-Point Blade
Photo Paper	287	
Printable Fabric	249	
Silk, Bonded	285	Bonded Fabric Blade
Stencil Film – 0.4mm	341	

MATERIALS: WHAT CAN I CUT WITH MY CRICUT MAKER OR ... | 73

Tattoo Paper	312	
Vellum	277	Fine-Point Blade
Washi Sheet	139	
Wax Paper	139	

That was a long list! Well, if you're impressed with that, wait till you see the list of materials you can cut with a Cricut Maker.

CRICUT MAKER - COMPATIBLE MATERIALS

Here's the list of materials that are compatible with this pro-level model.

Material	Cut Pressure Setting	Blade Type
Acetate	319	
Adhesive Foil	121	Fine-Point Blade
Adhesive Foil, Matte	161	
Adhesive Sheet, Double-sided	250	
Aluminum Foil	78	Deep-Point Blade
Art/Illustration Board	750	
Balsa – 1.6mm	200	Knife Blade
Balsa – 2.4mm	300	
Bamboo Fabric	1041	Rotary Blade
Basswood – 1.6mm	750	

Basswood – 0.8mm	381	Knife Blade
Birch, Permanent Adhesive	350	Fine-Point Blade
Boucle	2365	Rotary Blade
Broadcloth	1370	
Burlap	3163	
Burnout Velvet	1410	Rotary Blade
Calico	1608	
Cambric	1785	
Canvas	1925	
Carbon Fiber	138	Fine-Point Blade
Cardstock (For intricate cuts)	182	
Cardstock, Adhesive-Backed	314	
Cashmere	1424	Rotary Blade
Cereal Box	348	Deep-Point Blade
Chalkboard Vinyl	175	Fine-Point Blade
Challis	1040	

Chambray	1680	
Chantilly Lace	1540	
Charmeuse Satin	1695	Rotary blade
Chiffon	684	
Chintz	1505	
Clear Printable Sticker Paper	229	
Colored Duct Tape	120	Fine-Point Blade
Construction Paper	168	
Copy Paper	113	
Corduroy	1725	Rotary Blade
Corrugated Paper	329	Deep-Point Blade
Cotton, Bonded	286	Bonded Fabric Blade
Crepe Charmeuse	1430	
Crepe de Chine	1610	
Crepe Paper	958	
Crepe-back Satin	2000	

Damask	1838	Rotary Blade
Delicate Fabric (e.g. Tulle)	800	
Denim	1943	
Dotted Swiss	1339	
Double Cloth	1438	
Double Knit	1605	
Duck Cloth	2110	
Everyday Iron-On	118	Fine-Point Blade
Everyday Iron-On Mosaic	230	
Express Iron-On	118	
Faux Fur	2050	Rotary Blade
Faux Leather (Paper Thin)	260	Fine-Point Blade
Faux Suede	1885	
Felt, Acrylic Fabric	1995	Rotary Blade
Felt, Glitter Bonded	2214	
Felt, Stiff	175	Fine-Point Blade

Material	Setting	Blade
Felt, Wool Bonded	275	Fine-Point Blade
Foil Acetate	292	
Foil Iron-On	138	
Foil Paper – 0.36mm	274	
Foil Poster Board	333	
Freezer Paper	128	
Gabardine	1854	Rotary Blade
Garment Leather (0.8mm – 1.6mm)	300	Knife Blade
Gauze	335	Rotary Blade
Gel Sheet	335	Deep-Point Blade
Genuine Leather	325	
Glitter Cardstock	263	Fine-Point Blade
Glitter Craft Foam	214	
Glitter Duct Tape	271	
Glitter Iron-On	205	

Glitter Vinyl	75	
Grocery Bag	215	
Grosgrain	2228	Rotary Blade
Handmade Paper	1729	
Heavy Fabric (e.g. Denim)	3200	
Interlock Knit	1926	
Jacquard	1953	Rotary Blade
Jersey	1520	
Kevlar	2217	
Khaki	2110	
Kraft Board	278	
Kraft Cardstock	270	Fine-Point Blade
Laser Copy Paper	126	
Light Cardstock (163gsm)	238	
Light Chipboard – 0.37mm	285	
Light Cotton	1750	Rotary Blade

Light Fabrics (e.g. Silk), Bonded	175	Bonded Fabric Blade
Linen	2148	Rotary Blade
Lycra	1250	
Magnetic Sheet – 0.6mm	358	Deep-Point Blade
Matte Vinyl	134	Fine-Point Blade
Metal – 40gauge thin copper	256	
Metallic Iron-On Mosaic	325	
Microfiber	1708	Rotary Blade
Monk's Cloth	3295	Rotary Blade
Muslin	1595	
Ottoman	2023	
Panne Velvet	1425	
Printable Fabric	199	Fine-Point Blade
Sandblast Stencil	190	Deep-Point Blade
Sequined	2570	Rotary Blade
Shimmer Leather – 1mm	253	

Material	Count	Blade
Sticky Note	193	Fine-Point Blade
Sticker Paper, Removable	106	
Tissue Paper	1308	Rotary Blade
Tooling Leather	400	Knife Blade
Velvet Upholstery	2134	Rotary Blade
Waffle Cloth	2338	
Washi Sheet	85	Fine-Point Blade
Wax Paper	169	
Window Cling	99	
Wool Crepe	1174	Rotary Blade
Ziberline	1883	

I bet you're amazed by the materials list that a Cricut Maker can cut. And get this, this isn't even the full list! So, you can imagine how many more projects you can make with just one model.

In the next chapter, I'll guide you on setting up your Cricut machine so you can be on your way to creating many awesome crafts and projects!

4

HOW TO MAINTAIN YOUR CRICUT

In this chapter, I'll share with you the right steps to maintain your Cricut. I'll talk about how you can clean your machine, as well as the steps to clean your tools and accessories. Remember that your machine and tools are your best friend, so you need to take good care of them!

Let's take a look at how you can maintain your Cricut machine.

CLEANING YOUR CRICUT MACHINE

For many first time Cricut owners, you may be a little wary about the right way to clean your machine. So here are the steps you can follow in cleaning your machine. Soon, your machine will not only look as clean as a whistle, but you can also help to ensure that you can use the machine for a long time!

1. 1Always disconnect your Cricut from power before cleaning it.
2. Wipe your machine with a soft cloth. You may use glass cleaner spray to clean your machine. Spray the cleaner onto the cloth first, and then wipe your machine down.
3. At times, you may notice static electricity, causing dust and paper particles to collect. You can wipe this away with a dry anti-static cloth. You can also use a lens blower to remove the debris and particles gently.
4. Use a Q-tip, cotton swab, or a soft cloth to remove the grease if there's any buildup in its carriage track. See below for instructions on how to re-grease your carriage track after cleaning the buildup.
5. NEVER use acetone to clean your Cricut. The harsh chemical can ruin and damage the plastic surface of your machine.

RE-GREASING YOUR CRICUT MACHINE

1. Always make sure your machine is disconnected from the power source.

2. Gently push the Cut Smart cartridge to the left.

The Cut Smart cartridge is where you place your blades, tools, or pens 105 - Photo via: Babysaver

3. Using a tissue or a soft cloth, clean the Cut Smart cartridge, wiping it around the entire bar. The carriage bar is the rod where the cartridge slides on.

106 - Wipe the carriage bar with a soft, clean cloth Photo via: Rafael Gutierrez

4. Now gently push the Cut Smart cartridge to the right.

5. Repeat Step 3.

6. Gently move the Cut Smart cartridge to the center of your machine.

7. Open your lubricant packet. Squeeze a small amount onto a Q-tip.

8. Apply light coating of grease around the bar on both sides of the Cut Smart cartridge. You don't have to cover the entire bar, but enough to create a ¼ ring of grease on each side of the bar.

HOW TO MAINTAIN YOUR CRICUT | 83

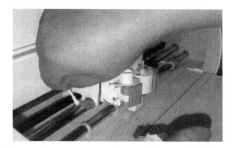

107 - Remember not to use too much grease Photo via: Rafael Gutierrez

9. Slowly and gently move the Cut Smart cartridge to the left and then move it back all the way to the right. This ensures an even coating of the grease along the entire bar.

10. Remove any excess grease buildup at the ends of the bar.

Make sure you use Cricut lubrication as other third-party lubricants may not be suitable or might be too harsh for your machine.

HOW TO MAINTAIN YOUR CRICUT MATS

There's a simple way to clean your mat and also to bring back its adhesive. Let's take a look at how to maintain your Cricut mats.

Cleaning your mats

To ensure that your mat can last a long time, I strongly recommend that you clean your mat after three to four cuts.

108 - Just a light layer of soap is enough to help clean your Cricut mat Photo via: Craft and Courage

1. Start by removing large debris from your mat using a tweezer. Be careful not to scar or scratch your mat with the tweezer. You can also use a lint roller to remove that hard-to-get debris. REMEMBER: Don't pick out the debris or residue with your fingernails.

109 - Make sure you use suitable scraper to clean debris off your mat Photo via: Amazon

2. Follow these steps to wash and clean your mat:

   a. Keep your mat flat by placing it on a firm surface and place your mat in the sink or tub.
   b. Run lukewarm water over your mat.

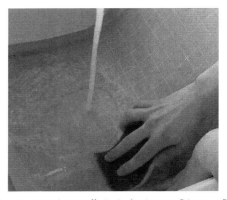

110 - Using warm water is more effective in cleaning your Cricut mats Photo via: DIY Ways

   c. Use a hard-bristle brush and scrub your mat in a circular motion to remove final traces of debris. You don't need to use soap. However, if you want to, make sure you only use a very mild soap (I usually use my kid's bath gel). Harsh or strong soap can strip away your mat's adhesive. Don't squeeze the soap directly onto your mat. Instead, mix the soap into a bowl of water to thin it and dip your brush into this bowl.
   d. Rinse with lukewarm water to remove debris and/or suds.

HOW TO MAINTAIN YOUR CRICUT | 85

111 - Make sure you use alcohol-free wipes to pre-clean your Cricut mats Photo via: Reddit

3. After cleaning your mat, DON'T pat it with a towel or a paper towel. This will only cause debris and particles to stick again. Dry your mat on a wire rack in a well-ventilated area. You don't have to dry it out in the sun, just in an airy room will suffice.

How to make your Cricut mat sticky again

Your Cricut mat is self-adhesive to help your materials stick. Over time, your mat can lose its stickiness. However, there's an easy way to bring back the stickiness.

One of the easiest ways to do this is to clean your mat often. However, if whenever you feel your mat is not as sticky as it once was, follow these steps to restore its adhesive.

There are two ways that I use to restore my mats. We'll take a look at both methods.

Using a glue pen

1. Use a jumbo tip glue pen because the sponge tip is wide enough to cover your mat evenly and in broad strokes. Many glue pens have colored glue substance but they'll turn clear once they dry.

112 - My favorite glue pen to restore my Cricut mat adhesive Photo via: Amazon

2. You need to prime the glue pen to ensure it flows smoothly through the sponge tip when you restick your Cricut mat. Gently press your glue pen against any surface until you see the sponge tip turn darker or blue.

3. Once your mat is completely dry, apply the glue in even broad strokes using the gridlines inside the mat as a guide. Ensure you don't get any glue on the edge of your mat because the sticky edges can damage the cutting unit.

113 - Keep your glue pen vertical against the mat for even application Photo via: Cut, Cut, Craft!

4. Allow your mat to dry for at least 30 minutes, and all the glue has turned clear. If you feel the mat is too sticky, you can lightly use a lint roller to remove excess glue.

5. Make sure you wait several hours for the glue to completely dry before covering your mat with its protective film. This way, your film won't be permanently stuck to your mat.

Using an adhesive spray

1. Use masking tape to tape your mat onto a wide and flat surface. The masking tape is important in preventing the spray from covering your whole mat.

2. Follow the instruction of your adhesive spray. Spray your mat as evenly as possible.

3. Allow appropriate drying time as per instructions on the can.

114 - My favorite adhesive sprays to restick my Cricut mats, all available from Amazon Photo via: Amazon

HOW TO MAINTAIN YOUR CRICUT | 87

MAINTAINING YOUR CRICUT BLADES

Your Cricut blades can last a long time with proper care. Regardless of how frequently you use your Cricut blades or what types of materials you cut, your Cricut blades are made to last a very long time with proper care maintenance.

In this section, we'll take a look at several aspects of Cricut blade maintenance so you can keep your blade sharp and in good condition.

Keeping your blades sharp

Cricut blades are made from premium carbide steel. This means they're made to last longer, stay sharp longer than average blades, and are made to withstand wear and tear. However, there are still certain things you can do to ensure that your Cricut blades stay sharp.

Instead of replacing a new blade every time it becomes dull, try these tricks instead:

1. Sharpen your blades by poking them in and out into a balled-up aluminum foil. The ball of aluminum foil can help remove fine bits of paper particles and debris, and vinyl residual. You can do this after every 2 - 4 cuts to maintain the sharpness of your blades.

115 - I find that the aluminum foil ball is one of the most effective ways to keep your Cricut blades sharp Photo via: SVG & Me

2. You can also sharpen it by making cuts on an aluminum foil sheet. Spread a piece of foil on your mat and cut simple designs on it. This technique can remove all debris and particles on your blade too.

Note: Be careful when you remove the blade from the housing. You may feel the blades aren't sharp enough for you to cut your materials, but they're still sharp enough to cut you if handled carelessly.

Storing your Cricut blades the right way

The most important thing when it comes to storing your Cricut blades is to make sure that they're safe. As mentioned, the blades are sharp, and you wouldn't want to injure yourself or anyone.

Cricut has a built-in compartment for you to store all your blades and tools. Everything is made easy for you, so you don't have to fuss over little things. You can safely store your blades in this compartment. This way, not only are they safe and secure from prying fingers, but you also won't lose them!

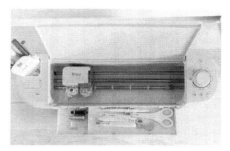

116 - Use the compartment in front of your Cricut machine to store your blades and tools Photo via: Daydream Into Reality

You can also design your own compartment or storing unit for your blades. Since you already have a Cricut machine, why not use it to create a personalized and customized container for your blades!

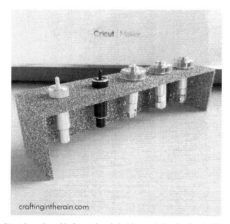

117 - I just love these blades and tools holder made by Stephanie! Photo via: Crafting In The Rain

Where to buy Cricut replacement blades

Of course, the main source will be the Cricut shop. They have all blades, tips, housing, tools, and accessories that you need and can use with your Cricut machine. But many other marketplaces offer original Cricut replacement blades.

My other favorite places to hunt for Cricut blades are:

- Amazon
- Michaels
- JOANN

Cricut often runs offers and sales for their blades and other tools and accessories, but the products are often out of stock. I find that JOANN and Michaels run much more attractive promotions and discounts on their Cricut products.

Shop around a little before you buy any Cricut blades or other accessories.

Frequent Cricut blades problems

In my experience of using Cricut, there aren't really problems when it comes to Cricut blades. Once the issues are identified, they're often caused by mistakes or oversights, and not the blades or the machine itself.

To understand how you can manage and avoid Cricut blades "problems," I'll share some of the most common issues faced by Cricut users.

Bad cuts

This is one of the most common complaints about Cricut blades. Typically, bad cuts happen because of various or multiple reasons. Before you blame the blades or the machine, you'll need to identify why you are getting "bad cuts."

Here are some common "bad cuts" situations that you may face:

Cutting Issues	Possible cause	Solution
Blade not cutting	<ul><li>Force too low</li><li>Insufficient blade exposure</li><li>The blade is too high</li><li>Chipped blade</li></ul>	<ul><li>Increase cutting force</li><li>Check blade exposure</li><li>Adjust the blade's height</li><li>Replace blade</li></ul>
Tearing	<ul><li>Too much blade exposure</li><li>Force too high</li><li>Condition of materials</li><li>Incompatible/unsuitable material</li></ul>	<ul><li>Check blade exposure</li><li>Lower cutting force</li><li>Check materials are not exposed to humidity/Use fresh material</li><li>Check if the material is compatible with the blade</li></ul>
Partial cuts	<ul><li>Force too low</li><li>Blade too close to the material</li><li>Material not stable</li><li>Need more than one pass</li><li>Incorrect speed</li></ul>	<ul><li>Increase cutting force</li><li>Adjust the blade's height</li><li>Check mat's stickiness</li><li>Perform multiple passes</li><li>Adjust speed</li></ul>

Bad setting

Your Cricut machine has the Smart Set dial, a material selection knob that you can point to the materials you're cutting. However, relying on this alone is not enough. I find it best to use the material settings in Design Space cut screen rather than using the Smart Set dial. Turn your dial to Custom and select your material from the dropdown list in the Cut Screen before cutting.

If you still can't get the accurate and clean-cut you're looking for; you can manually increase the pressure in your Design Space screen.

WORD OF CAUTION: Don't change the setting more than twice at a time. Changing the pressure setting may change the way your machine cuts materials in the future. I won't recommend this as your first solution because, as mentioned earlier, you may need some time to get used to your machine's default pressure setting before you can make customized settings.

Machine not detecting blade

This is another common issue faced by Cricut users.

If it ever happens to you, go through the steps below to resolve this situation:

1. First, check you have the right tool in Clamp B, as stated in Design Space. If you don't have the right suggested tool, remove your cutting mat to return to the Project Review screen. Select the Edit Tools link to choose a different tool. Now make sure the tool you selected from the screen matches the one you install in the clamp.
2. If the problem persists, remove the tool from Clamp B. Clean the tool sensor using a lens blower (don't squeeze too hard, you just need a gentle puff of air). You can also use a soft microfiber cloth to clean the sensor.
3. If all else fails, there's one last thing you can try before you call Cricut's careline. You can uninstall and reinstall Design Space on your desktop or smartphone. Go through the steps that I've shared earlier about setting up Design Space and see if your machine can detect your blades or tools now.

Maintaining your Cricut machine takes a lot of TLC.

You may need to spend about half a day cleaning your mats, blades, and machines. However, the extra effort you put in into maintaining your Cricut will be worth the time.

In the final chapter of this book, I'll go through some of the most frequently asked questions about anything Cricut.

CONCLUSION

This has been a fun ride!

The Cricut machines have long been a trusted and reliable companion for many crafters, and I think you can see why. Here, I've only so far shared some projects that you can do, but I'm sure there are tons more that you can create!

This first book introduces everything Cricut to understand what it is and what it can do to help your crafting. It can feel a little overwhelming as a beginner because it seems like there's so much to know about Cricut. But if you think this book has helped you understand this amazing die-cutting machine, why not leave a review on Amazon to let others know about it too!

The details I've shared about each Cricut model in Chapter 1 should help you understand what each model is for and what it can do. Remember to assess several things such as project size, materials you usually use, and frequency of usage before you go out and buy any Cricut model.

I know in the early stages of using Cricut, you might feel a little swamped with all the information about Cricut tools and accessories. This is why I shared everything I know in Chapter Two about using the right tools and accessories. Take your time to get comfortable using a Cricut machine first before investing in more tools and accessories.

To ensure your Cricut lasts a long time, using the right tools is not the only important thing. Make sure you cut the right material with the right blade at the right setting. This is why knowing suitable and compatible materials is important. Remember the list of materials in Chapter Three, and you'll be all right.

Another important aspect to remember is regular maintenance. As I've shown in Chapter Four, besides regularly maintaining your machine, make sure you practice proper care in cleaning your machine. Your Cricut machine is built to last, but it can go a long way if you take the time to regularly clean and maintain it.

CONCLUSION

I have shared everything I know in this book for you, and I can't wait to see what you can create with your Cricut machines. There's only so much I can share and tell because now that you're geared up with the knowledge of what a Cricut can do, it's time for you to go out and make something awesome! The more you use your machine, the more you're able to explore its possibilities. And from this, you can discover more things to do to improve your crafting skills as well as start expanding your home business.

If you find this book helpful and fun, please leave a kind review on Amazon. I would love to hear your thoughts on how much this book has helped you understand everything about Cricut.

REFERENCES

Amazon, (Image 112) 'Bulk Buy: Zig 2 Way Glue Pen Bulk Jumbo Tip' Available at: My Book

Amazon, (114) 'Spray glue' Available at: https://www.amazon.com/s?k=spray+glue&ref=nb_sb_noss_2

Anastasia, A., 28 October 2020, (Image 15) 'Gift Box Happy Birthday' *Unsplash*. Available at: https://unsplash.com/photos/UjLx301mSl0?utm_source=unsplash&utm_medium=referral&utm_content=creditShareLink

Andersen, S., 08 February 2019, (Image 69) 'What Is The Cricut BrightPad and What Can I Use It For' *Tastefully Frugal*. Available at: https://tastefullyfrugal.org/2019/02/what-is-the-cricut-brightpad-and-what-can-i-use-it-for.html

Brothers, 31 March 2014, (Image 119) 'Brother ScanNCut - The world's first home & hobby cutting machine' Available at: https://www.youtube.com/watch?v=hjQlm5O_hIg

Burris, L., 17 August 2020, (Image 53, 54) '7 Ways To Store Cricut Pens And Markers' *Organized-ish*. Available at: https://www.lelaburris.com/store-cricut-pens/

Cerruti, C., (Image 14) 'Cricut Crafts: Lace Greeting Cards' *Creative Bug*. Available at: https://www.creativebug.com/classseries/cricut-classes-on-creativebug/cricut-crafts-make-lacey-greeting-cards

Clark, F., and Clark, K., 01 November 2019, 'What DIY Projects Can I Make with My Cricut? 50+ Creatives Ideas' *Clarks Condensed*. Available at: https://www.clarkscondensed.com/diy/cricut/what-diy-projects-can-i-make-with-my-cricut/

Courtney, H., 22 January 2020, (Image 109) 'Cricut Beginner Tips: How to Clean Cricut Cutting Mats' *Craft eCorner*. Available at: https://www.craft-e-corner.com/blogs/project-inspiration/how-to-clean-cricut-cutting-mats

94 | REFERENCES

Craft and Courage (Image 108) 'Best way to clean your Cricut mat' Available at: https://craftandcourage.com/best-way-to-clean-your-cricut-mat/

Cricut (Image 11) - Available at: https://cricut.com/en_us/cricut-easypress

Cricut (Image 118) - Available at: https://cricut.com

Cricut, (Image 34 - 46) 'All About Cricut Blades and Machine' Available at: https://help.cricut.com/hc/en-us/articles/360009432294-All-About-Cricut-Blades-and-Machine-Tools

Cricut (Image 90 - 104) 'Downloading and Installing Design Space' Available at: https://help.cricut.com/hc/en-us/articles/360009428814-Downloading-and-Installing-Design-Space

Cricut (Image 73 - 87) 'How do I pair my Cricut Explore or Cricut Maker machine via Bluetooth?' Available at: https://help.cricut.com/hc/en-us/articles/360009380974-How-do-I-pair-my-Cricut-Explore-or-Cricut-Maker-machine-via-Bluetooth-

Cricut (Image 123) 'How do I use the Contour function in Design Space?' Available at: https://help.cricut.com/hc/en-us/articles/360009508613-How-do-I-use-the-Contour-function-in-Design-Space-

Cricut, (Image 48 - 51) 'Materials and Pens' Available at: https://help.cricut.com/hc/en-us/sections/360007239514-Materials-and-Pens

Cricut Blog (Image 3, 4) - Available at: https://inspiration.cricut.com/bold-cricut-explore-air-2-family/

Cricut Infusible Ink™ (Image 55) - Available at: https://cricut.com/en_us/infusible-ink

Cricut Inspiration (Image 2) - Available at: https://inspiration.cricut.com/meet_cricut_joy/

Cricut Inspiration (Image 9) - Available at: https://www.youtube.com/watch?app=desktop&v=FnQR3AWFYA0

Cricut Joy (Image 1, 13, 16, 17, 18, 19, 20, 47) - Available at: https://cricut.com/en_us/cricut-joy

Cricut Learn (Image 125) - Available at: https://learn.cricut.com/maker/getting-started

Cricut Maker (Image 7) - Available at: https://cricut.com/en_us/cricut-maker

Cricut Mats (Image 59 - 62, 64 - 67) - Available at: https://cricut.com/en_us/essentials/machine-tools/cutting-machine.html

Cricut Pinterest (Image 6) - Available at: https://www.pinterest.com/Cricut/_created/

Cricut Shop (Image 121) 'Basic Tool Set' Available at: https://cricut.com/en_us/cricut-basic-tool-set.html

Daydream into Reality (Image 127) - Available at: https://www.daydreamintoreality.com

Daydream into Reality, 20 April 2019, (Image 58, 63) 'Cricut Mats Differences Guide - Everything You Need to Know' Available at: https://www.daydreamintoreality.com/cricut-mats/#Light_Grip_Blue_Mat

Daydream into Reality, 12 November 2019, (Image 10) 'What is the Cricut EasyPress Mini? Is it worth it' Available at: https://www.daydreamintoreality.com/cricut-easypress-mini/

REFERENCES | 95

Daydream into Reality, 24 December 2018, (Image 116) 'Cricut Blades Differences Guide - Everything You Need to Know' Available at: https://www.daydreamintoreality.com/cricut-blades/#How_to_Care_for_my_Cricut_Blades

Dennis, C., 14 March 2020, 'What is a Cricut machine and what does it do?' *The DIY Mommy*. Available at: https://thediymommy.com/what-is-a-cricut-machine-and-what-does-it-do/

Design Cricut (Image 71, 72, 88, 89) - Available at: https://design.cricut.com

Devriend, T., 15 August 2018, (Image 8) 'How to use the new Cricut EasyPress 2!' *AuntieTay YouTube*. Available at: https://www.youtube.com/watch?app=desktop&v=FnQR3AWFYA0

DIY Ways. (Image 110) Available at: https://diyways.com/how-to-clean-and-restick-cricut-mats/

Elizabeth, M., 21 April 2011, (Image 25) 'Spring or Easter Like Scrapbook Inspiration!' *Above Rubies*. Available at: https://www.aboverubiesstudio.com/videos-and-projects/cricut/spring-or-easter-like-scrapbook-inspiration/3422/

Ejmont, J., (Image 70)'Beginner's Guide on How To Use a Cricut Machine', *The Best Vinyl Cutter*. Available at: https://www.thebestvinylcutters.com/how-to-use-a-cricut-machine/

Fekitoa, L., 18 July 2020, (Image 31) 'Make Customized Wrapping Paper With Stamps and Your Cricut' *Lindsay Bake, Make, Create*. Available at: https://seelindsay.com/make-stamps-cricut/

Fields, A., 07 October 2018, (Image 113) 'How To Clean Your Cricut Cutting Mat (And Restick It After)' *Cut, Cut, Craft!* Available at: https://www.cutcutcraft.com/clean-cricut-mat/

Gathercole, J., 02 September 2019, (Image 21) 'Halloween Trick or Treat.' *Unsplash*. Available at: https://unsplash.com/photos/gS44KF7OzGs?utm_source=unsplash&utm_medium=referral&utm_content=creditShareLink

Griffth, L., '17 Frighteningly Good Halloween DIYs' *Lia Griffith*. Available at: https://liagriffith.com/17-frighteningly-good-halloween-diys/

George, C., (Image 128) *Hey, Let's Make Stuff!* Available at: https://heyletsmakestuff.com

George, C., 05 June 2019, (Image 68) 'How to use the Cricut tool set' *Hey, Let's Make Stuff!* Available at: https://heyletsmakestuff.com/cricut-tool-set/

Griffith, L., (Image 21) 'Gorgeous DIY Projects' Available at: https://liagriffith.com

Gutierrez, R., 19 March 2018, (Image 106, 107) 'Cricut Grease: Application' *YouTube*. Available at: https://www.youtube.com/watch?v=y0pCOPosAhw

Hamilton, M., 27 February 2017, (Image 105) 'Cricut Explore Air 2 Review: Everything You Need to Know' *Babysavers*. Available at: https://www.babysavers.com/cricut-explore-air-2-review/

Hofstadt, M., 21 August 2019, 'How To Restick Your Cricut Mat' *Vinyl Cutting Machines*. Available at: https://vinylcuttingmachines.net/how-to/restick-your-cricut-mat/#how_to_restick_cricut_mat

96 | REFERENCES

Holden, A., 29 July 2020, (Image 120) 'The Ultimate Guide to Cricut Blades for Every Machine' *The Country Chic Cottage*. Available at: https://www.thecountrychiccottage.net/guide-to-cricut-blades/

Holder, C., 12 October 2017, (Image 28) 'How to Make a Cozy Fall Pillow Using the Cricut Explore' *Keys to Inspiration*. Available at: https://www.keystoinspiration.com/make-cozy-fall-pillow-using-cricut-explore/

Joann, (Image 15) 'Cricut Mini - Elegant Thank You Card and Envelope' Available at: https://www.joann.com/cricut-mini---elegant-thank-you-card-and-envelope/4331271P134.html

Kirsten, A., 02 April 2019, (Image 52) 'How to Use Any Pen with Your Cricut Machine: Cricut Pens Tutorial' *Abbi Kirsten Collections*. Available at: https://www.abbikirstencollections.com/2019/04/cricutpenstutorial.html

Kundin, H., 13 December 2017, 'The Cricut Maker Machine - What's New and What Can It Do?' *Happiness is Homemade*. Available at: https://www.happinessishomemade.net/the-cricut-maker-machine-whats-new-and-what-can-it-do/

Kutsch, L., 18 March 2019, (Image 29) 'Make Up Bag with Cricut EasyPress and a Giveaway' *Lori's Scrappy Bunch - Create Your World*. Available at: https://lorisscrappybunch.blogspot.com/2019/03/make-up-bag-with-cricut-easy-press-and.html

Lugovnin, M., 15 April 2020, 'Beige pillow with inscriptions on the bed' *Unsplash*. Available at: https://unsplash.com/photos/uzKhxFX-Quo?utm_source=unsplash&utm_medium=referral&utm_content=creditShareLink

Lynn, L., 04 June 2019, (Image 56) 'New: Cricut Infusible Ink is Awesome' *Craft Box Girls*. Available at: https://craftboxgirls.com/blogs/articles/new-cricut-infusible-ink-is-awesome

Makers Gonna Learn, (Image 27) 'How to use Cricut printable iron-on' Available at: https://makersgonnalearn.com/how-to-use-cricut-printable-iron-on/

Maker, J., (Image 126) *Jennifer Maker*, Available at: https://jennifermaker.com

Marx, J., 08 January 2018, "Cricut Writing and Pen Tutorial: Tips and Tricks' *JenniferMaker*. Available at: https://jennifermaker.com/cricut-writing-tutorial-tips-tricks-fonts/

McGuinness, D., 01 August 2020, '16 Things to Make With a Cricut Machine' *Cafe Mom*. Available at: https://cafemom.com/lifestyle/226468-things-to-make-with-cricut/354960-iron_on_t_shirt

Media, S., 10 March 2019, (Image 56) 'Earrings and tote bag 3' *Unsplash*. Available at: https://unsplash.com/photos/ZduWSICPFF0?utm_source=unsplash&utm_medium=referral&utm_content=creditShareLink

Media, S., 04 August 2019, (Image 27) *Unsplash*. Available at: https://unsplash.com/photos/qeDcKFADdp8/info

Parkinson, A., 12 May 2020, (Image 119) 'Silhouette CAMEO die cutting machine review' Available at: https://www.toptenreviews.com/die-cutting-machines-silhouette-cameo-review

Paxman, S., 20 August 2018, (Image 117) 'Cricut Maker Tool Holder' *Crafting In The Rain*. Available at: https://craftingintherain.com/cricut-maker-tool-holder/

REFERENCES | 97

Pettiford, E., & Turley, J., 16 May 2017, (Image 23) 'How to Make a Fun Paper Flower Crown' *Bespoke Bride*. Available at: https://www.bespoke-bride.com/2017/05/16/how-to-make-a-fun-paper-flower-crown/

Poole, M., 04 June 2018, *Unsplash*. Available at: https://unsplash.com/photos/JmEBAMLhuxw?utm_source=unsplash&utm_medium=referral&utm_content=creditShareLink

Pure, J., 16 November 2020, *Unsplash*. Available at: https://unsplash.com/photos/qr-glQASy0Y/info

Reddit, 2017, (Image 111) 'Cleaning my cricut mats with Clorox wipes' Available at: https://www.reddit.com/r/cricut/comments/70pvio/cleaning_my_cricut_mats_with_clorox_wipes/

Roe, J., 28 June 2018, (Image 124) 'What is Cricut Access?' *Cricut Blog*. Available at: https://inspiration.cricut.com/what-is-cricut-access/

Schensted, L., 12 February 2015, (Image 5) 'Cricut Explore Air Debut!' *Lisa is Busy Nerding*. Available at: http://www.lisaisbusynerding.com/2015/02/cricut-explore-air-debut.html

Scraps, S., 14 July 2020, (Image 24) '8 Sizzling Summer Scrapbook Ideas!' *Scrapbooking Store*. Available at: https://blog.scrapbookingstore.com/8-sizzling-summer-scrapbook-ideas/

Sikkema, K., 30 November 2016, 'Paper Snowflakes' *Unsplash*. Available at: https://unsplash.com/photos/QlL_MIF7Xjc?utm_source=unsplash&utm_medium=referral&utm_content=creditShareLink

Simple Made Pretty, 12 March 2020, (Image 32) 'How to Make Stamps Using Cricut' Available at: https://simplemadepretty.com/make-stamps-using-cricut/

Sparmo, J., 10 January 2020, (Image 26) 'Free Cricut Scrapbook Layouts' *Cookies, Coffee & Crafts*. Available at: http://www.cookiescoffeeandcrafts.com/free-cricut-scrapbook-layouts/

SVG and Me, 16 May 2018, (Image 115) '15 Cricut Hacks You Probably Didn't Know About' *SVG and Me*. Available at: https://svgandme.com/cricut-hacks/

Thomas, M., 09 March 2016, (Image 30) 'DIY Stamped Swaddle Blanket' *Designs by Miss Mandee*. Available at: https://www.designsbymissmandee.com/2016/03/diy-stamped-swaddle-blankets/

Thomas, M., 15 January 2019, 'Die Cut Quills - Harry Potter Cut Files' *Designs by Miss Mandee*. Available at: https://www.designsbymissmandee.com/2019/01/die-cut-quills/

Thomas, M., 08 August 2019, (Image 24) 'Die Cut School Bus - Back To School Cut Files' *Designs by Miss Mandee*. Available at: https://www.designsbymissmandee.com/2019/08/die-cut-school-bus/

Thomas, M., 01 December 2020, 'Angel Luminaries - Christmas Cut Files' *Designs by Miss Mandee*. Available at: https://www.designsbymissmandee.com/2020/12/angel-luminaries/

Thomas, M., 07 January 2021, 'Woven Baskets - Die Cut Baskets' *Designs by Miss Mandee*. Available at: https://www.designsbymissmandee.com/2021/01/woven-baskets/

Thomas, M., 20 January 2021, 'Die Cut Peacock' *Designs by Miss Mandee*. Available at: https://www.designsbymissmandee.com/2021/01/die-cut-peacock/

REFERENCES

Viscount, M., 18 December 2018, (Image 12) 'Cricut EasyPress 2 Review - All Your Burning Questions Answered' *Silhouette School.* Available at: https://www.silhouetteschoolblog.com/2018/12/cricut-easypress-2-review-all-your.html

Weathers, E., 01 December 2020, 'Cricut EasyPress Review - Is it the Best Cricut Heat Press?' *Smarter Crafting.* Available at: https://freshlypickedblog.com/cricut-easy-press-review/

Writer, S., 16 April 2020, (Image 122) 'Cricut Accessories | Tools, Paper, Iron-On & More' *Hip2Save.* Available at: https://hip2save.com/2020/04/16/40-off-cricut-accessories-free-shipping-tools-paper-iron-on-more/

Wulf, D., 03 November 2015, (Image 22)'Make Your Own Paper Christmas Ornaments' *DIY Inspired.* Available at: https://diyinspired.com/diy-paper-christmas-ornaments/

BOOK 2

CRICUT DESIGN SPACE FOR 2021 AND BEYOND: THE BEGINNER'S STEP-BY-STEP GUIDE TO MASTERING CRICUT DESIGN SPACE IN JUST 21 DAYS

© Copyright 2021 - All rights reserved.

It is not legal to reproduce, duplicate, or transmit any part of this document in either electronic means or in printed format. Recording of this publication is strictly prohibited and any storage of this document is not allowed unless with written permission from the publisher except for the use of brief quotations in a book review.

CLAIM YOUR BONUS

The Cricut Tool Kit
This is what you'll get in this Free tool kit:

1. Over 100 beautiful **SVG Files** that will spark your creativity

2. The Cricut Supplies Cheatsheet, with the most essential supplies you'll need for your first project

3. Access to our private Facebook group where you get to meet like-minded Cricut lovers and get tons of project ideas and tons of **free SVGs**

To claim your tool kit simply Click Here. Or Copy and paste this link into your browser: https://productiveplans.activehosted.com/f/7

INTRODUCTION

Up till now, I don't know what glued Sophia and me together. Our friendship started at elementary school, and we clicked right from day one. Eight years ago, she called to let me know that her wedding would be held in Los Angeles in August. And, right there, I made a promise to her that I would design her a Cricut Flower Coloring Page Card. The project isn't complicated at all, and I've seen people craft some adorable Cricut flower coloring page cards. "Perfect. You know I have never hidden my love for Cricut-made designs," she said. I assured her I would do all it takes to make her wedding a memorable one. She'd invited all her friends to witness the design's crafting, and all eyes were fixed on me to deliver the project.

I was prepared to customize the design and spice it up with several elements. Yes, what I saw people do in the past had just one element, but I felt I could design something more appealing and enticing. I knew I would clip some parts together, position my cuts on the cutting mat, and fasten Linetype selections, especially Draw and Score. Also, I should sustain my spacing when the design runs through the Cut Preview Screen once I tap the "Go" button. I cut the project many times, but it was a big mess all the time. I kept trying this until I eventually gave up, disappointing my friend, Sophia, and myself. I later realized that the reason behind the big failure is that I didn't use the "Attach" tool, and I didn't know that at the time. How am I supposed to know? I was just a beginner then.

No matter how small a Design Space skill or tool appears, learn to master it to avoid loss of time, money, customers, or other crafting issues. If you want to create an Iron-On Vinyl t-shirt, for example, you need to ready your cutting machine, pressing iron, cutting mat, scissors, and a pick or any weeding tools. Apart from the t-shirt you intend to work with, your ironing board, parchment paper, or Teflon sheet should be made available.

Fine, you spent the money to assemble the materials, but you're sweating so hard to find a suitable image or font to use on Design Space for over an hour. Perhaps, you want to combine two projects on the same mat, but it seems nothing is working. Eventually, you gave up, and you never started the project.

INTRODUCTION

Just imagine how you'll feel if you're confident with your Design Space research skills and you know for sure that you can easily locate the perfect image for your project under five minutes, or even combine images and play with fonts as if it was an easy game.

What exactly should you look out for in this book? Look out for all you need to up your skills in using Design Space to create amazing DIYs effortlessly.

- I will tell you exactly what Design Space is and walk you through the process of downloading, installing, and launching Design Space on your PC, iOS, and Android device, step by step, until you master it.
- You will learn how to set up your Design Space account and how to use it.
- I will show you the essential tools and functions of Design Space, one after the other. You'll also understand Design Space Canvas Area and how to use the tools and functions proficiently.
- I will walk you through several Cricut projects, step by step, until you can create your own designs.
- You will learn how to upload, edit, and customize images in Design Space, as well as where and how to get great image cartridges for your design.
- I will show you some fantastic tips in Advanced Design Space, and you'll have no problem creating a unique Cricut project straight away.
- I will show you some tricks to maximizing the Cricut Design Space and pushing up your design skills a bit.

So, you have nothing to worry about. Did I say there's nothing to worry about? No. You surely need to worry about your concentration and determination to master Cricut Design Space. Put all your focus on what you are about to learn in this book because that's all you need to bring your passion to life.

Your journey to creating your first Cricut project takes us to Design Space and how to launch it, our focus in Chapter One.

I hope you enjoy the book.

1

DESIGN SPACE AND HOW TO LAUNCH IT

Cricut Design Space is a design app for cutting unique projects. It works fine on Cricut Explore, Joy, and Maker machines. With this software, you can create your Cricut project from scratch or browse a few ready-to-make projects via Design Space, the Cricut software platform. Design activities, such as editing, adding fonts and images, and changing colors occur within the Design Space. If you want to be a pro-Cricut designer, master the Design Space.

Downloading and Installing Cricut Design Space

Design Space works fine on iOS or Android devices and Windows or Mac computers. It makes no difference whether you're using a PC or mobile device; you can download and install the application on either. Here, I will run through the process of downloading and installing Design Space on Windows, Mac, iOS, and Android. Just make sure your internet connection is stable before you attempt downloading or signing in to the Design Space application.

DOWNLOADING, INSTALLING, AND LAUNCHING DESIGN SPACE ON:

WINDOWS PC

Feel free to download and install the Design Space software on your Windows PC. Follow these simple steps to download, install, and launch Cricut Design Space on your Windows PC.

106 | BOOK 2

1. Use your internet browser to navigate design.cricut.com and select "Download."

Cricut Design Space download page for Windows PC

2. Double-click the downloaded file to start the installation process. A window will pop up, asking whether you trust the source of the application.

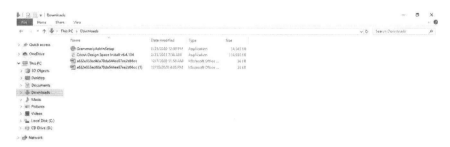

Downloaded file on the Computer Download Folder

3. Click the option to confirm that you trust the application to progress the installation process.

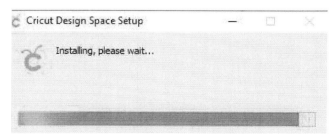

Cricut installation in progress

DESIGN SPACE AND HOW TO LAUNCH IT | 107

4. Use your Cricut ID and password to sign in to the application. You will see the Design Space icon on your Desktop screen.

Cricut Sign in page

5. Right-click on the Design Space icon and select "Pin to Taskbar," or simply drag the icon to your Taskbar, where you can easily use it.

You have successfully downloaded and installed Design Space on your Windows PC. Launch it to begin the process of creating your first Cricut project.

MAC PC

Users of Mac PC are not left out. They can download the Cricut software, install, and run it via their PC. How? Follow these simple steps to download, install, and launch Cricut Design Space on your Mac PC.

1. Navigate design.cricut.com via your internet browser and click on "Download."

Cricut Design Space download page for Mac PC

2. Double-click the downloaded file to start the installation process.

Downloaded file on the Computer Download Folder

3. Move the Cricut icon to your Application folder to continue the installation process. Design Space app will be added to the Applications folder of your Desktop automatically.

4. Double-click the app to launch the program on your Desktop. Drag the app to your Desktop to create a Design Space shortcut.

DESIGN SPACE AND HOW TO LAUNCH IT | 109

Design Space and other Programs shortcuts on PC

5. Click on "Open" when you get a Mac notice, asking whether the downloaded Design Space app should open or not.

Opening Design Space app on Mac PC

6. Use your Cricut ID and password to sign in to the application.

Cricut Sign in page

You just downloaded and installed Cricut Design Space on your Mac PC. Launch it and start your first Cricut project.

IOS

Cricut Design Space can work on a compatible iOS. Once it is installed as an app on your iOS, you can start creating your unique projects, with or without the internet. But, before you make the downloads, make sure your iOS is compatible with the software. Check the compatibility of your iOS by logging in to www.design.cricut.com and check the list of compatible iOS devices. Once you get the green light, just follow these simple steps to download the app for your iOS device. It takes less than five minutes to complete the process.

1. Go to the home screen of your iOS device > click and open the App Store > find the Cricut Design Space.

DESIGN SPACE AND HOW TO LAUNCH IT | 111

Cricut Design Space and other apps on iOS home screen

The app comes with a white square and a green "C" logo.

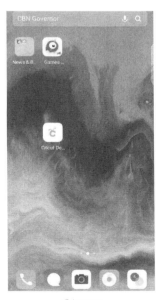

Cricut app

112 | BOOK 2

2. Click on "Get" to download the app. You may need to use your iTunes password to verify and complete the download.

Design Space app will launch automatically as soon as the download completes, and you'll be asked to finish the "New Machine Setup" or navigate the "App Overview." Pick your choice or simply click on "X" if you don't want to select either option.

3. Use your Cricut ID and password to sign in (or create one if you don't have any) and start your first Cricut project.

Cricut Sign in page

ANDROID DEVICE

Cricut Design Space can work as a regular app on your Android device. Again, like the iOS device, not all Android phones are supported on the Cricut platform. So, initiate a check via the Cricut website to determine if your Android version gets the pass mark. Once it is installed, you can start creating Cricut projects, with or without the internet. Just follow these simple steps to download the app for your Android device.

1. Navigate Google Play Store to find Cricut Design Space. The app has a white square and a green "C" logo.

DESIGN SPACE AND HOW TO LAUNCH IT | 113

Cricut Design Space download page for Android Device

2. Download and install the app by clicking the "Install" button. Wait for the installation process to complete. The app will launch automatically as soon as the installation process is done.

3. Open the app > sign in with your Cricut ID and password > create your first project.

Cricut Sign in page

What type of Cricut machine did you purchase—EasyPress 2, Maker, or Explore? No issues. Pay careful attention to the following options while setting up, registering, or updating your newly purchased Cricut machine.

Design Space page for setting up, registering, or updating Cricut machines

- Calibration: Here, you get to see the calibration options for Knife Blade, Rotary Blade, and Print Then Cut.
- Manage Custom Materials: Click this option to access the material settings for the already connected Cricut machine. Change the name if you want but carefully check each material's Blade Type, Multi-Cut settings, and Cut Pressure. Feel free to scroll down to the bottom of the list to see the "Add a New Material" option. If you like the settings, fine. If not, change everything.
- Update Firmware: Click here to update the firmware of your installed Cricut machine. It is not a one-time thing. From time to time, update the firmware. If you don't update, you'll have issues running the software or application effortlessly on your device.
- Account Details: Use this option to access your order history, payment details, membership details, and other account information.
- Link Cartridges: Click this option to link your Cricut cartridges, if you have any. But you can do this on your iOS or Android device, except Desktop or laptop.

UNINSTALL CRICUT DESIGN SPACE

You can uninstall Design Space applications from your mobile device or PC. Yes, you might want to troubleshoot your device or uninstall the app permanently for personal reasons. Follow these simple steps to uninstall the Cricut Design Space.

1. Close the Design Space app on your Desktop. The application will not uninstall if it is open while you're running the uninstallation process.

2. Click open the Start icon > search Programs for Add or remove programs > open Apps & features window.

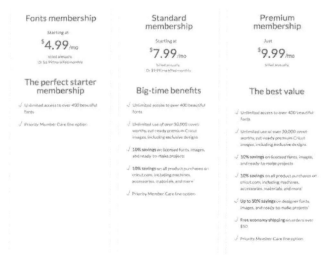

Add or remove programs page on PC

DESIGN SPACE AND HOW TO LAUNCH IT | 115

3. Search for Cricut to select "Cricut Design Space," and tap the "Uninstall" option.

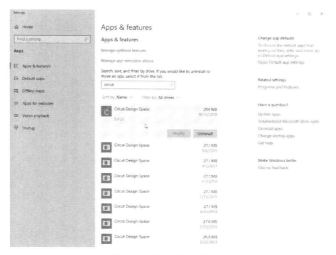

Removing Cricut Design Space

4. A warning will pop up, indicating whether you want to uninstall your Cricut Design Space. Confirm your action.

Program removal caution page

The system will finish the uninstallation process. Feel free to restart your PC, iOS, or Android device.

UNWRAP AND SET UP YOUR NEWLY PURCHASED CRICUT MACHINE

Congratulations on getting your personal Cricut Maker, Joy, or Explore machine. Now you can start creating your own unique Cricut projects once you unwrap and set up the newly purchased machine, and you can do this in under 10 minutes! How can I do this? No issues. Just follow these simple steps to unwrap and set up your Cricut machine.

A box of newly-bought Cricut Maker

Step 1. Open the Box: Carefully open the box and pick the "Welcome" packet. The packet lies flat on the Cricut machine, and it houses all the goodies you need to create your first Cricut project, including a USB cable and rotary blade. If you find the USB cable, dig deeper, as it is usually the last item in the box.

Just lift the machine from its protective cardboard to locate the power cord and the two cutting mats you will use to craft your first Cricut project.

Cricut EasyPress 2 placed on a flat surface

Step 2. Unwrap the Cricut Machine: Remove the machine from its protective filmy wrapper and cellophane. Carefully remove the foam layer. Then, take off the Styrofoam that protects the inner housing of the machine.

Step 3. Unwrap the Supplies: Unwrap the rotary blade, its cover, and the USB cable, as well as other components of the machine. You don't need to worry about the fine point pen. Why? The manufacturer has already incorporated it with the machine's housing.

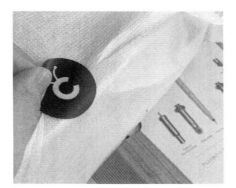

Cricut Maker machine being removed from its box

Step 4. Navigate cricut.com/setup: Get ready to sort out the whole show's technical aspects since you have unwrapped your Cricut machine and its goodies. Cricut's website is user-friendly, and you won't have any problems running through its entire webpage.

Just navigate cricut.com/setup via your PC and follow the instructions on the web page to set up your Cricut machine. You will be asked to install Cricut Design Space. Once this is done, sign up to the app to get a Cricut ID. You should be logged in to the app now.

Should that not be the case, log in with your Cricut ID and password to perfect the final steps. Plug the USB cord and the power cord.

An overview of the Cricut Maker machine

Step 5. Claim Your Goodies: You get Cricut Access free of charge for one month when you set up a newly purchased Cricut machine. You will get rich Cricut fonts, projects, and Ready-to-Make files for one full month.

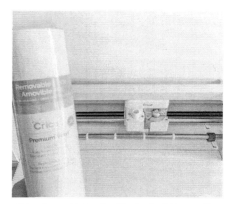

Cricut Removable Premium Vinyl and a Maker machine

Feel free to use all the tools on your Cricut Maker, Cricut Joy, or Cricut Explore to replicate the fantastic projects on Cricut Access.

Step 6. Start Your First Project: You have successfully unwrapped and set up your Cricut. What's next? Start your first project. Do you have any projects at heart? Design it straight away if you have any. If not, don't panic.

Cricut Design Space has a significant amount of fun projects for beginners. Learn how to create these simple projects to up your skills and master your Cricut tools.

CRICUT ACCESS

Cricut Access is a pathway to unique Cricut images, fonts, graphics, and ready-to-make projects. It is a paid membership platform where you get significant discounts on physical products, licensed fonts, photos, and other design aids that could make your next Cricut Design Space project a huge success. With over 400 fonts, 1,000 ready-to-make projects, and 30,000 non-licensed images, Cricut Access has become a potent force in the world of creative design.

Are you a frequent crafter or a newbie in the crafting business? Do you want to up your crafting skills? Would you appreciate fantastic Cricut project ideas or ready-to-make projects to start from scratch? If your answer to these questions is yes, you need to subscribe to Cricut Access. Not only does Cricut Access save a significant amount of money and time for crafters, but it also ensures that you get quality images and fonts for your projects, especially licensed ones. It saves time because you don't have to surf the internet for images and fonts all-day. Cricut Access has all you need to create amazing Design Space projects.

How do I get Cricut Access? Just navigate to design.cricut.com and use your Cricut ID and password to log in. Click on Cricut Access. Pay keen attention to the instructions on the pop-up screen. Then start your free trial. The whole process shouldn't take more than five minutes, depending on your internet connection.

So, whether you are a regular crafter or a newbie, I will guide you through the process of selecting the right Cricut Access subscription. But before then, check the right panel of your

DESIGN SPACE AND HOW TO LAUNCH IT | 119

Design Space to study and understand the following options, or you'll have issues using or subscribing for the perfect Cricut Access plan.

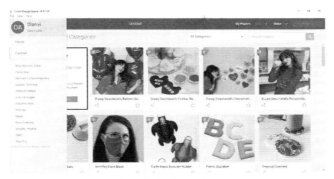

Cricut Design Space options

- Settings: A click on Setting allows you to alter the settings of the Design Space grid. So, depending on what works best for you, feel free to use Imperial or Metric units of measure.
- Legal: Just click this option to get permission to use Cricut Access. Here, you get to see Cricut Access Terms of Use, and you may need to accept these terms before you can proceed.
- New Features: Click this option to see information on new Cricut features. If you click and nothing pops up, no worries. Information on new or additional features for subscribers will be reeled out to you as they pop up.
- Country: Use this option to change your country. Choose Canada, the United States, the United Kingdom, or whichever is your country of domicile.
- Help: Click this button to link up with the Help Center. Here, you get to see helpful FAQs, troubleshooting aids, how-to articles, and lots more.
- Sign Out: Just click on this button to sign out from Design Space. To log in again, you will need to supply your Cricut ID and password.
- Feedback: A click on this option pops up a feedback form. Fill the form to leave feedback or comments for Support. The feedback option is invaluable when you have some troubleshooting issues. Just click the option, and help will come via the Support team.

CRICUT ACCESS PLANS

Cricut Access, a monthly or yearly paid membership platform, offers instant access to a vast library of images, fonts, and ready-to-cut Cricut projects. What's your thought about Cricut Access? Sure, you should know whether you really need Cricut Access or not. Take your time to make your decision. But while you think about it, let me quickly show you the available Cricut plans, their similarities and differences, and a tip on how to opt for the right plan. Did I say the right plan? No. Feel free to opt for the plan that works best for your designs.

Here are the features of all Cricut Access plans:

- Unlimited access to over 50,000 images, graphics, and ready-to-cut projects.
- Unlimited access to over 400 fonts.
- 10 percent savings on every physical product you purchase through cricut.com.
- 10 percent savings on each image, cartridge, and ready-to-cut projects on fonts purchased from leading brands such as Hello Kitty, Disney, and Sesame Street.
- 50 percent less wait time for members who call the Cricut Care Line.

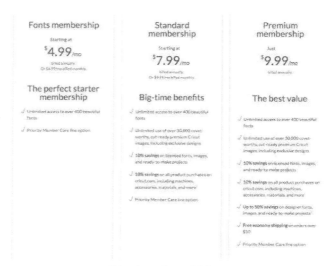

Cricut Access plans and their cost

Fine. Now, let's see the available Cricut Access plans and the comparative advantage each plan has over the other.

Perfect Starter Plan

Just like its name, the perfect starter plan is designed for newbies or crafters who want to see how Cricut Access works. For example, someone just informed you that Cricut Access houses all the materials you need to create your favorite project. Still, the whole idea seems impossible, or you felt you shouldn't invest so much money in it. Should this be your situation right now, opt for the perfect starter plan. Sure, you can back out if the plan makes little or no sense to you. How much will I pay for this plan? You need $9.99 to use the plan for one full month.

Annual Plan

The Annual Plan benefits are the same as the Perfect Starter Plan. Billing is per year but, instead of paying $9.99 per month, you will pay a flat rate of $7.99. Be prepared to pay a one-year commitment fee totaling $95.88 upfront to use this plan.

DESIGN SPACE AND HOW TO LAUNCH IT | 121

Cricut Access annual plan

Premium Plan

Apart from the general perks open to Cricut Access subscribers, the Premium Plan offers these significant values to subscribers.

Cricut Access premium plan

- Up to 50 percent discounts on Ready-to-Make or ready-to-cut projects, licensed fonts, images, and graphics. But this huge discount does not apply to big brands such as Hello Kitty, Disney, and Sesame Street.
- Free Economy Shipping awaits you once you spend over $9.99 on orders.

Just like the Annual Plan, if you're on this Cricut Access plan you will be billed annually. Be prepared to pay $119.88 upfront, totaling $9.99 per month.

I would pick the Perfect Starter Pack as my favorite Cricut Access plan because I can cancel it at any time. Still, if you love what you get, you can upgrade to get more benefits or values. Feel free to pick the plan that suits your projects.

DIFFERENCE BETWEEN CRICUT ACCESS, CRICUT CARTRIDGES, LICENSED FONTS, AND IMAGES

Have you ever wondered about the differences between Cricut Access, Cartridges, Fonts, and Images? You are not alone. So many crafters, especially beginners, have asked similar questions in the last few years. No worries. Here, you get to see what each term actually means.

With Cricut Access, you get to purchase separate images, fonts, and Ready-to-Make projects in varied packages, while a cartridge is a collection of special fonts, graphics, and images. Nothing differentiates Cricut Access from Cricut Cartridges more than their manner of purchase. While you have to opt for membership to purchase your favorite items on Cricut Access, a one-time purchase is required on Cricut Cartridges. You can use the one-time purchase at any point while running your Cricut Design Space project.

Again, Cricut Access does not have all cartridges. Sure, with Cricut Access, you get to see a vast library of elements. Yet, Disney, Sesame Street, and other well-known licensed illustrations, including fonts and ready-to-cut projects, are not available.

How do I get these images and fonts? No worries. You could get them separately or get the cartridge that has them. Cricut partners with leading brands, such as Hello Kitty, Disney, and Sesame Street, to make sure you have the right materials to create beautiful Cricut projects using your favorite characters.

Pros and Cons of Cricut Access

Are you still wondering about getting Cricut Access or not? A look at Cricut Access Pros and Cons should help you take a stand.

Pros

- It can boost your creativity and encourage you to work more with your Cricut machine.
- It has a few easy-to-learn fun projects for your development.
- You get access to amazing materials, machines, and accessories via cricut.com, and you will make extra savings in the process.
- You don't need prior experience or knowledge to design a beautiful project if you have Cricut Access.
- You have access to any of your favorite designs or projects throughout the year.
- Access to functional graphics and fonts. All the materials you get on Cricut Access will do the intended jobs perfectly once you follow the stated instructions.

Cons

- It has a recurring payment structure. Once payment ceases, access to used fonts, graphics, and Ready-to-Make projects, including other freebies, will be blocked.
- Cricut Access fonts, images, and graphics can only be used in the Cricut Design Space. Some crafters often integrate these fonts, graphics, and images with what is available in Adobe Illustrator or Inkscape. Yet, it doesn't always come out clean and unique.

ALTERNATIVE OPTIONS FOR CRICUT ACCESS

Cricut Design Space can be used to cut your projects. You can cut your personal files and upload them, even if you don't have Cricut Access. Creating the files or uploading them isn't the problem, but where can you locate these files? No worries. Pay keen attention to these options.

- Take advantage of the Cricut Design Space weekly Free Cuts.
- Hundreds of free Cricut project tutorials are available for download online. Freely use Pinterest or Google to search for these online tutorials.
- Etsy, TheHungryJpeg, and Creative Market have numerous options for your next project, although you'll need to purchase them.

Create and design your Cuts from scratch. Sure, this takes time and patience. It is similar to learning a new skill from scratch, but you'll soon get used to it. Feel free to use creative software like Illustrator or Inkscape to create a top-notch design.

Learning Design Space, inside out, and how to launch it was your first significant step to understanding how to work with the software. But there are more laps to cover before you can create your first Cricut project. One of these laps is "Mastering the Design Space Canvas Area," our focus in the next chapter.

2

MASTERING THE DESIGN SPACE CANVAS AREA

Are you having difficulty mastering the Cricut Design Space, or you're not sure how to get started with it? No worries! Here, you get to see the Icons and Panels of the Design Space and what you can do with them. True, a new skill or hobby can look difficult or intimidating at first. Yet, if you learn it from scratch to find out what each panel or icon stands for, you will master how to create amazing projects with the Cricut Design Space. Don't be in a hurry to jump from one project to the other. No! Know your work area if you want to up your creativity a bit.

WHAT EXACTLY IS THE CANVAS AREA?

Cricut Design Space Canvas Area is the center of creativity since that's where you will design your projects and add or edit text and images. It houses the tools you need to upload desired fonts and images and touch up or organize your project. Also, via the Canvas Area, you can purchase and use Cartridges, Cricut premium fonts and photos, and Cricut Access. Master how to use each icon in the Cricut Design Space Canvas Area, or you will have issues crafting your favorite projects.

How can I work with the Cricut Design Space? Just create your account. Log in to the account via CANVAS, the Design Space window, and start a new project or edit an existing one. It's that simple! Did I say simple? Not really. There are a few options, tasks, and buttons to punch to get the job done perfectly, but don't worry. I will take you through the process step-by-step until you learn how best to use all the Icons and Panels on the Canvas Area. I'll split the Canvas into four parts and four colors to make the whole thing straightforward and easy-to-understand.

- Top Panel (Yellow)— Editing Area
- Right Panel (Purple)— Layers Panel
- Left Panel (Blue)— Insert Area

MASTERING THE DESIGN SPACE CANVAS AREA | 125

- Canvas Area (Green)

It's time to master the Cricut Design Space. Are you ready?

THE CRICUT DESIGN SPACE TOP PANEL

Use the Canvas Area top panel to edit and arrange the elements of your project. Tap the panel to opt for your favorite font, varying font sizes, align designs, and perfect lots of functions. The top panel houses two sub-panels—one for saving, naming, and cutting projects, the other to edit and control other elements within the canvas area. Here are the two sub-panels.

Name Your Project and Cut It

Right from the Canvas Area, use this panel to navigate your profile and projects. Check out and master the options under this sub-panel.

Canvas Area Top Panel: Name Your Project and Cut It

- **Toggle Menu:** A click on this button pops up a menu, totally different from the Canvas. You can use this button to navigate your profile, change your photo, calibrate your blades and machine, manage your account details and Cricut Access subscriptions, and update your device software or firmware.

Feel free to use the settings option to alter the measurements and visibility of your canvas.

Design Space Toggle Menu

126 | BOOK 2

- **Project Name:** All projects come with no definite title. But you have to give specific names to all the projects you work on within the Design Space Canvas Area, or you'll have issues working on multiple projects at the same time. So, once you add an image, a shape, or any other element, create a name for your project.
- **My Projects:** Here is a link to the library where all your projects are stored. A click on "My Projects" takes you directly to the library you already created. Let's assume you want to edit or cut an existing project. Just click this option to locate the project and effect necessary adjustments.
- **Save:** You get to see this option once you add an image, a shape, or other elements to your canvas area. The Cricut software can save your elements automatically. Save your projects step-by-step to avoid any technical issues.
- **Maker or Explore Machine:** Opt for Cricut Joy, Maker, or Cricut Explore Machine once you have carefully considered the type of machine you intend to work with, especially if you're working with multiple Cricut machines. While the Cricut Maker houses many options, you need to point out those that are perfect for your chosen machine. For example, if you switch ON the Explore option while working with a Cricut Maker, the Maker tools will stay deactivated.

Cricut machine options on Design Space

- **Make It:** Click "Make it" once you have successfully uploaded your files and set them to cut. A click on "Make it" will divide your projects by mats, based on the colors of the projects. Also, via this option, you can cut many projects one after the other.

EDITING MENU

Use this button to arrange, organize, and edit both images and fonts. A click on the editing menu will pop up any of these options.

- **Undo & Redo:** We make lots of mistakes when we create our designs. But, with these fantastic buttons, we can easily correct our errors. Tap Undo if you just created something out of point or Redo if you mistakenly deleted or modified an element.

Design Space undo and redo project options

- **Linetype & Fill:** With this option, your machine gets to know the blades and tools you're using for the project. Depending on your machine, feel free to select Joy, Explore, or Maker on the top part of your CANVAS, also known as the window.

Linetype and Fill options on Design Space

- **Linetype:** A click on this option tells your machine the tool you plan to use to cut your project. Only eight options are available at the moment—Cut, Engrave, Score, Draw, Deboss, Perf, Foil, and Wave. You get to see all these options if you are using a Cricut Maker. But, with an Explore, you'll have four options—Foil, Score, Cut, and Draw. Last but far from least, users of Cricut Joy can only use Cut and Draw options. Fine. Let's see these tools, one after the other.

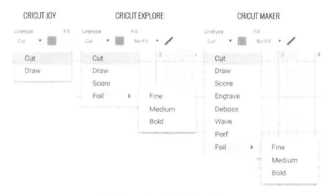

Linetype options for Cricut machines

A comparative analysis of Cricut Joy, Explore, and Maker Linetype

- **Cut:** All the elements you add to the canvas will use cut because it's the default line type. Still, you can alter this arrangement by uploading PNG or JPEG images to your Canvas. Feel free to vary the fill of the uploaded elements once you select the Cut option.
- **Draw:** Use this line type to write on your project. Opt for one of the Cricut pens on display but make sure it has the right color for your design. You can use a third-party adapter if you have one. A click on a design will outline your canvas area layers. Again, use this tool to instruct your Cricut to draw or write on your design once you tap the "Make it" button.
- **Score:** Use this line type to make your designs scored or dashed. Right there on the left panel lies the scoring line. Once in use, and you tap "Make it," your Cricut will score or dash your materials, rather than cutting the design. But if you are determined to work on these kinds of projects, ready the scoring wheel (compatible with the Cricut Maker only) or the scoring stylus.

- **Engrave:** Use this line type to engrave all kinds of materials. Would you like to engrave your anodized aluminum or aluminum sheets with monograms? Just click on "Engrave" to get the job done.
- **Deboss:** Use "Deboss" to create unique designs and customize your designs. Also, the debossing tip helps push the material into the machine while you creatively design unique projects.
- **Wave:** A wavy effect will aid the aesthetics of your final cuts and designs. Rather than using the rotary or any regular straight-line cutter, opt for this tool. Again, with this tool in use, you get to create a striking effect in your design.
- **Perf:** With this tool in use, you get to create small, uniformed, and beautiful lines on your materials, similar to the crisp aesthetic effects you see on tear-out cards, coupons, raffle tickets, and other great designs out there.
- **Foil:** Use this newest Cricut tool to spice up your project with adorable foil finishes. Feel free to opt for fine, medium, or bold finishes when you're using this linetype option.
- **Fill:** Here is a printing or pattern option. You activate "Fill" once you make "Cut"your linetype option. Deactivating "Fill" means no printing is required. If the "Fill" is activated and you click on "Make it," your files move straight to the printer, and the Cricut will run the cutting process. Should you be working on patterns, simply use those on the Cricut or add your favorite patterns.

Fill options on Cricut Design Space

- **Select All:** It is hard to select all the elements one after the other if you want to move them to the canvass area, especially when working on a project with multiple layers. Instead, click on "Select All" to simply perform the task.

MASTERING THE DESIGN SPACE CANVAS AREA | 129

Design Space 'select all' icon

- **Edit:** Use the "Edit" icon to cut or copy items from the canvas, and paste the items in the desired canvas area. A click on the icon will open a drop-down menu of cut, copy, and paste. Just select one or more items in the canvas area to activate the cut or copy option. Once you copy or cut the selected items, the paste option is activated.

Design Space 'edit' icon options

- **Align:** Aid aesthetics by selecting two or more items in the canvas area and aligning the design as you want. A click on "Align" opens options such as "Align Left," "Center Horizontal," "Align Right," "Align Top," "Center Vertically," "Align Bottom," and "Center."

Design Space Align options

While "Align Left" will push your elements to the left, "Center Horizontal" will align the elements horizontally and center both images and text. A click on "Align Right" will move the elements to the right, but "Align Top" tilts selected items up a bit.

Click on "Center Vertically" to align your selected items vertically or "Align Bottom" if you want to push selected items down. "Center" is a cool option if you're going to balance the design vertically and horizontally.

- **Distribute:** It's hard to manually create uniform spacing between elements within the canvas area. If you manage to work it out, lots of time will be wasted, and the output won't be 100% accurate. Just click on "Distribute" to avoid this nightmare. Again, remember to select three or more items to activate the "Distribute" option. A click on this option will pop up "Distribute Horizontally" and "Distribute Vertically."
- **Arrange:** If you are working with several designs, texts, and images, the new items you add will sit in front of other items already uploaded, which could mess up the design. You can avoid this by using the "Arrange" option. A click on "Arrange" will open "Send to Back," "Move Backward," "Move Forward," and "Sent to Front" options.

MASTERING THE DESIGN SPACE CANVAS AREA | 131

Design Space Arrange options

Click "Send to Back" to push selected items to the back or "Move Backward" to move the items one step to the back. Move the items one step forward by clicking on "Move Forward" even as a click on "Sent to Front" will push the items to the front.

- **Flip:** Use this option to reflect or examine the outlook of your design. A click on "Flip" will pop up two options—Flip Horizontal and Flip Vertical. Click on "Flip Horizontal" to reflect your design in the form of a mirror, and it's perfect if you are creating designs with wings. With "Flip Vertical," your design will have a water-like reflection, and it's great if you want to create a striking shadow effect for the design.

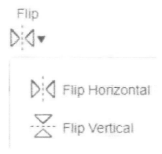

Flip icon on Design Space

- **Size:** Every item you create has size but, feel free to modify your creations' size and measurement.

Size icon on Design Space

How? Click the "Size" option to increase or reduce your image, text, or design.

- **Rotate:** Use this function to rotate added items to preferred angles and positions.

Rotate icon on Design Space

- **Position:** A click on "Position" will show you the location of your elements and designs on the canvas area. Use the tool to move your elements as you want. But, since this tool is a bit advanced, you can settle for the alignment tools.

Position icon on Design Space

- **Font:** Click on "Font" to opt for the one suitable for your project. Simply watch out for fonts with green "A" if you're working with Cricut Access. You don't have Cricut Access? No issues. Use the fonts on your system.
- **Style:** Feel free to change the form of your font once it is picked. A click on "Style" will open these options—Regular, Bold, Italic, and Bold Italic. Use the option that works best for your designs.

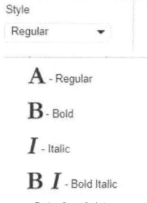

Design Space Style icon

- **Alignment:** Yes, the alignment here is totally different from the one already discussed.

MASTERING THE DESIGN SPACE CANVAS AREA | 133

Alignment options on Design Space

Use this alignment to adjust your paragraphs. Just tap "Left," "Center," or "Right" to keep your paragraphs properly aligned.

- **Curve:** This option can aid your creativity with text. Just use the slider to curve your text upwards or inwards until you get the perfect shape you love!

Curve icon on Design Space

- **Advance:** Don't let the name or the drop-down menu scare you. No! You'll soon get to know that the "Advance" option is easy to use. Here is what you will see when you click the "Advance" option.

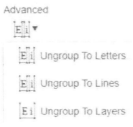

Design Space 'Advanced' icon

1. **Ungroup to Letters**: Sometimes, because of your design's nature, you need to modify all your characters to separate layers. Click on this option to do it effortlessly.
2. **Ungroup to Lines**: Use this option to separate each line in the paragraph. Once you finish typing the paragraph, highlight it, click on "Ungroup to Lines," and you will have separate adjustable lines. It's that simple.
3. **Ungroup to Layers**: Already considered the trickiest, you can't use "Ungroup to Layers" unless you're working with Multi-Layer fonts. Such fonts come with several layers, but you have to purchase them or simply use Cricut Access. Multi-Layer fonts look great on shadow or colored designs. What happens if you want just the font, not

the added layer? No worries! Select the text and tap "Ungroup to Layers" to separate each layer.

LEFT PANEL

Use the left panel to insert images, shapes, ready-to-cut projects, and other elements you want to cut. The left panel houses seven options.

- **New:** Use this option to either create a new project or replace an existing one on the canvas area. If you are working on a project and click on "New," a message on whether you want to replace your existing project will pop up. It is fine if you want to replace it but make sure you save the current project, or you will lose it.

Reminder to Save or replace project before a new one is initiated

- **Templates:** Use this option to gauge, test, or visualize your design outlook on a particular surface. Just know that this option doesn't add anything to the design.
- **Projects:** Go straight to "Projects" if you want to start cutting. Just select your project, customize it, click "Make it," pay keen attention to the cutting instructions, and finalize the process. Cricut Access members have lots of project options to pick from. Feel free to purchase the projects that work best for your Cricut machine.
- **Images:** Use images to beautify or personalize your projects. Search for as many photos as you want, provided they spice up or add value to your design. You won't have any issue finding amazing images if you have Cricut Access. Better still, you can purchase a few cartridges to access adorable images for your projects.

Design Space Image option

- **Text:** Click on "Text" to open "Add text here" anytime you want to use the program to type.

MASTERING THE DESIGN SPACE CANVAS AREA | 135

Text icon

- **Shapes:** Learn to create lovely projects with shapes. A click on "Shapes" will open seven great shapes: Triangle, Square, Pentagon, Star, Hexagon, Octagon, and Heart. Heart, the last option, isn't a shape but a wonderful tool to score your materials and design folds.

'Shapes' icon on Design Space

- **Uploads:** Upload the images and files once you're done with the project.

RIGHT PANEL

The right panel is all about layers. Each layer stands for one design or item on the canvas area. How intricate is the design you intend to create? Just know that the kinds of layers you need for a design depend on the project's complexity. Except for PNG and JPEG images, you can modify most layers. For example, you can convert a text layer to other forms of layers, although you won't be able to edit the text again. Here are the options you will see when you click on the Right Panel.

Design Space right panel

Group, Ungroup, Duplicate and Delete

- **Group:** Use this option if you're working on a complex project and want to group your layers. You need to group your layers to arrange the shapes, text, and images on the canvas area properly.
- **Ungroup:** Stylishly edit the size, font, position, and arrangement of the elements on the layer's panel or canvas area with this option.
- **Delete:** If there are any elements you don't want, select them and click "Delete."

In addition to the icons above, the Right Panel also houses these options.

Linetype or Fill

Check the items on your Layers Panel to know the particular Fill or Linetype in use. Is it Cut, Print, Wavy, Write, Perf, or Score? Feel free to check it out.

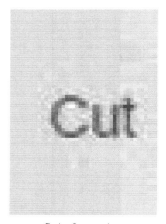

Design Space cut icon

Layer Visibility

Each layer on the layers panel has a little eye. Have you seen it? Fine. That's the visibility of the design. Don't be in a hurry to delete any item that looks odd. Hide the item by clicking the little eye. There's a cross mark on the eye once you hide the item.

Layer visibility icon

Blank Canvas

Sometimes, a particular design needs a color different from what you have on your canvas. Slightly adjust the color of the canvas by clicking the "Blank Canvas" option. Use this with Templates to unleash its appealing and enticing visual strength.

Blank canvas icon

Slice, Contour, Flatten, Weld, and Attach

Slice, weld, attach, flatten, and contour icons

1. **Slice:** Use the slice tool to cut your text, shapes, and other items to suitable sizes for your project. Just select the items you want to cut and click "Slice."
2. **Contour:** Feel free to hide design pieces you don't want by clicking the "Contour" tool. You can activate it if your design has unnecessary items or elements.
3. **Flatten:** Use this tool to offer additional support to the "Print" and "Cut Fill" options. The Print and Cut Fill options can address only a single layer at a time, unlike the "Flatten" tool. Just select the layers to print once you are done with the project and click "Flatten."
4. **Weld:** With this tool, nothing stops you from combining several shapes. Just select the shapes you want to combine, click "Weld," and see the new shape emerge. However, the back layer will determine the color of the newly formed shape.
5. **Attach:** Use this tool to group your Layers and connect shapes. If you connect shapes with "Attach," the attachment will remain firm even when you finally cut the project.

Color Sync

Each color on the canvas area stands for a specific material color. Just make sure that you use the color that adds value to your design. Nothing more!

Canvas Area

Here is where all your designs and elements are displayed. You need no special skill or intuition to use the canvas area.

Design Space Canvas area

- **Canvas Grid and Measurements:** A grid splits the canvas area. Those small squares on the grid help you see the cutting mat very clearly so that you can easily maximize the space. From inches to centimeters, feel free to alter the measurements and turn the grid off or on at will. Just click the top panel Toggle > Settings to either turn the grid on or off.
- **Selection:** This tool turns to blue when one or more layers are selected. Carefully modify the layers from all corners. Use the red x to delete unwanted layers or rotate the image from the canvas area's top-right corner. Yet, the editing menu has a rotate tool that can do this job perfectly. Use it.
- **Zoom in and Out:** Check the lower-left side of the canvas to locate the zoom in and out tool ("+" and "-" signs). Use the button to increase or decrease the design scale.

Great work! You just learned how to master the Design Space Canvas Area.

Yes, you just learned how to master the Design Canvas Area, the nerve of Cricut designs. A look at "Projects in Design Space," our focus in the next chapter, will push you a little bit close to your dream. See you there!

3

PROJECTS IN DESIGN SPACE

There are lots of unique projects to create. All you need to design one is creativity. Are you bereft of project ideas? No worries. Cricut project ideas flood the internet. Just type "Cricut project ideas" on Google, and you will be greeted with lots of attractive options. Feel free to replicate the ideas or create your projects from scratch. But, before you start to design your own unique project, pay keen attention to these strings of "how."

SAVING, OPENING, AND EDITING DESIGN SPACE PROJECT ON:

DESKTOP

Feel free to save your project when you add an element on the canvas area, or you will risk losing the whole thing should the Design Space crash. Yes, no autosave. Just save your changes every five or six minutes. Remember that the Save option lies in the window's top-right-hand corner, and it gets activated once an image is added. How do I save my project on Desktop?

- Place your first element on the canvas.
- Click Save > Name your project > Save.

140 | BOOK 2

'Save project as' option on Design Space

You will see a blue banner indicating that your project has been saved. Should you want to start a new project, save the existing one first.

Ready a clean and new canvas if you want to open an existing project. You won't be able to combine projects if the version of your Design Space is not 6.0.150. You can update your software via design.cricut.com, and you will combine your projects effortlessly. How can I combine projects? No worries. We will be covering that in Chapter Five, "Advanced Design Space Tips." Hopefully, you'll be able to combine projects on Cricut soon. Explore any of these two options to open your Design Space project on Desktop.

- Click on My Projects to access the project.
- Click on Projects > My Projects > select the project you want to open.

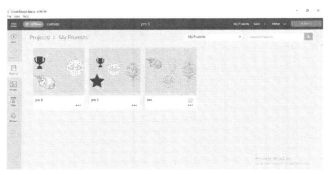

Saved projects on 'My projects'

You can use the "My Projects" option to edit, customize, cut, and delete an existing project. For example, a click on the three dots below each project allows you to delete the project.

It is normal to edit a project or change a few things in the project to enhance aesthetics. Effecting this on your Mac or Windows PC is quite easy and convenient, and it takes less than a minute, depending on your level of focus. Here is how to do it.

- Click Customize > select Edit > effect the changes.

PROJECTS IN DESIGN SPACE | 141

Using 'customize' option to edit a saved project

Editing requires little or no effort. Still, you need to be mindful of how you save the edited copy, especially if you want to keep the original project. Just click save if you don't need the original design. But, if you need it, click Save and select the "Save As" option to create a title for the edited copy.

APP

Home, Canvas, and Make are the three views on the Cricut Design Space App. Opening the app takes you directly to the "Home." Click "Canvas" or tap the big blue square with the "+" sign if you want to start a new project. Create at least one shape, text, or image to activate the "Save" option. Here is how to save your design.

Design Space views on mobile device

142 | BOOK 2

- Click Save icon > select Save to pop up a little window > type the name of the project > choose the destination to save the project.

'Save project' option on mobile Design Space

Opt for "Save to the Cloud" if the network connection in your area is reliable and you want to use your PC to access your projects. But if there no reliable internet in your area, select "Save to iPad/iPhone." Always remember that the "Save to iPad/iPhone" option will prevent you from accessing your projects via your PC. Save your changes every five or six minutes to avoid loss of work should the app crash.

What if I already have a project on my canvas, and I want to start another one afresh? No worries.

- Just save the existing project > click "Home" > tap "New Project."

Clean up your canvas first before you attempt to open an existing project. Click "Home" to pop up a drop-down menu and select the project's destination (Cloud or iPhone/iPad).

Should all your projects be in the Cloud, simply click "My Projects on the Cloud" from the drop-down menu.

A click on a project's "Customize" option allows you to edit and change the design the way you want. Just make sure you carefully save the original design, or you will risk losing it.

Using the 'customize' option to edit a project

PROJECTS IN DESIGN SPACE | 143

Simply save your project by clicking "Save," but you will override the original project if you used this method.

To keep the original project intact, click Save > Save As > create a name for the project and save the design.

SHARING YOUR DESIGN SPACE PROJECT ON:

IOS

Feel free to share your creative and amazing Cricut projects via apps to inspire other people. Sharing the projects is easy and convenient, and I will show you how to share your Design Space projects via Pinterest or Facebook straightaway.

- Log into design.cricut.com > supply your ID > password > click Sign In.
- Click on View all > select the project to share > click Share > add necessary information > select Add Details to activate the edit mode.

'View all' page on Cricut Design Space. Photo via Cricut. Cricut houses vital tools and tips you need to master Design Space.

- Locate the Photos header and click the "+" button to upload the project's image. Rotate the image with the rotate control and increase the image's size to 300%, using the zoom control.

'Photos header' page on Cricut Design Space. Photo via Cricut. Cricut houses vital tools and tips you need to master Design Space.

- Set the project toggle to "Visible to Others."
- Just make sure that the project name sounds nice and easy-to-understand, or other Cricut users would have issues decoding what the whole project is all about. Use popular tags to attract more Cricut users. Lots of amazing tags are on the list. Keep on typing to get great tags for your project. Each shared project can take up to fifteen tags.

Each shared project should have a brief description. Describe the project, tell us why you shared it, and for whom you created the project. A 500-word description is okay but don't forget to applaud makers or artists whose works inspired you. A few tips and instructions on how to replicate the project would be appreciated. Click Save once you finish adding the description.

An invitation to "Copy Project Link" will be displayed as soon as you finish sharing the project. Copy and paste the link on Pinterest or Facebook.

DESKTOP

Follow these simple steps to share your Design Space project on Mac or Windows desktop.

- Open your Design Space software > enter your ID > password > click Sign In.

PROJECTS IN DESIGN SPACE | 145

Design Space sign in page

Download and install the software if you don't have it on your PC.

- Locate Categories menu > click My Projects in the Cloud > select the project to share > tap the Share link under the project to activate the edit mode.

*'My projects in the cloud' page on Cricut Design Space. Photo via Cricut.
Cricut houses vital tools and tips you need to master Design Space.*

- Click the "+" button to upload the project's image > zoom the size to 300% with the pinch-to-zoom tool > position the image below the large rectangle on the page > create an easy-to-understand title for the project, and save.

Zooming and increasing the size of an image. Photo via Cricut. Cricut houses vital tools and tips you need to master Design Space.

Add handy tags to the project so that other Cricut users can easily find the shared project. Just continue typing letters to bring up tags for the project. Remember that each shared project can take up to fifteen tags.

Briefly describe the project. State why you're sharing it and whom it could benefit. Again, a few tips and instructions on creating the project from scratch will be great. The description should be at least 500 words. Decide "Who can view this project" and click "Done." An invitation to share the project link on Facebook or Pinterest will pop up. Copy and paste the link accordingly, or simply click "Done" if you're not willing to share the project.

USE DESIGN SPACE TEMPLATES

Design Space Templates offer you ample opportunity to take your design skills to another level. With a template, you can have a clear look and assessment of your final project. Here, I will show you how to use a Cricut Design Space template.

- Click "Templates" on the Canvas's left Design panel > run through the available templates > opt for your favorite template. Selected templates will appear on your Canvas screen, and you'll get a message indicating that the templates will be used for reference purposes only.

Design Space 'Templates' page

- View the template via the Template Edit bar. Click "Type" and "Size" options within the Template Edit bar to resize the template to suit your design. Check whether the templates come with the "Custom" option. You can use this option to vary the size of the template manually.

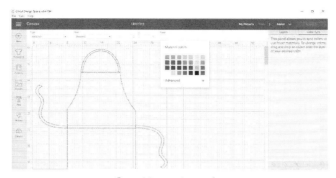

Customizing a project template

- Click "Template color swatch" under the Layers Panel to change the selected templates' color. A click on the "Template color swatch" will pop up several color options. Feel free to choose any of the custom or Basic palette colors. As soon as you make your color preference, your template will pick up the selected color.

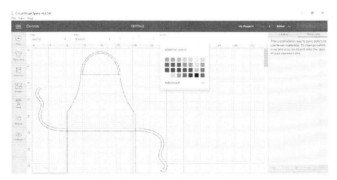

Design Space 'Template color swatch'

You can dismiss an already selected template. How? Click open the template and tap the "Delete" icon. Better still, click open the template and tap your keyboard's delete key.

USE READY-TO-MAKE DESIGN SPACE PROJECTS

Ready-to-Make projects such as home décor, fashion, and paper crafting designs from professional artists are readily available on Cricut Design Space. You can create these Design Space Ready-to-Make projects from scratch once you have the right supplies in place. Simply search through the Design Space Projects page to see numerous Ready-to-Make projects. Just click the Categories menu or the Search bar of your Mac or Windows PC to select your favorite project category. To do this, Design Space mobile app users should head straight to the "Home" tab to click their top screen.

Design Space ready-to-make project options

A click on a Ready-to-Make project opens all the things you need to design your own project, including the name of the project, its difficulty level and estimated completion time, materials required, instructions, and possible cost of the project.

Most Ready-to-Make projects are available to purchase. A purchase transfers ownership of the fonts, patterns, and images in the project to you. Then, since the project will be in your account permanently, you are free to use the resources in other projects.

PROJECTS IN DESIGN SPACE | 149

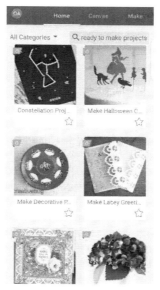

More ready-to-make projects

How can I create my own Ready-to-Make Design Space Project? No issues. Here is how to do it.

- Click the "Make It" button to launch the mat preview screen > tap the "Customize" button > add or adjust the images on the project file > click Save > tap Make It.

USE THE ATTACH TOOL

Have you ever wondered how you can cut your text and images exactly the way they appear on Design Space? Crafters, especially newbies, find this hard, but you can simply sort it out using the Cricut "Attach" tool. For example, center an image in a circle frame and click on "Align" and the "Go" button to cut the design. Yes, many crafters often do this, but the initial spacing on the cut preview screen will be completely undone. The image won't be cut as a single unit. The whole design will be messed up.

Has this happened to you before? No worries. Just select the images to cut > right-click > choose "Attach."

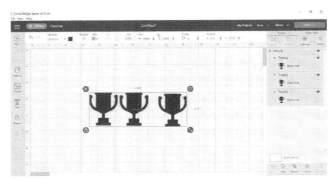

Using the 'attach' tool to cut images

It's that simple. "Attach" means that you simply want to attach a few selected shapes, text, or images to form a single element. "Attach" isn't "Group." Yes, you use "Group" to copy, size, and move items within the design screen but "Attach" does more than that. It ensures that once you click on the "Go" button, the selected items cut precisely the way you designed them.

Why should I use the "Attach" tool? You want to save time transferring your image(s) unit by unit, don't you? With the "Attach" tool, you can attach your images and cut them as a single element, weeding excess vinyl with little or no effort. Again, your spacing and other design elements will stay intact.

You are getting there gradually. Soon, you will create your first Cricut project. Get ready to learn how to use images in Design Space. That is what we will explore in the next chapter.

4

USING IMAGES IN DESIGN SPACE

Feel free to add images to aid the aesthetics of your Cricut projects. Lots of images are available for download in the Cricut Image Library. Interestingly, with the Cricut Design Space, you can use an image to create a project before purchasing the image. You can buy the image if it sits properly or adds value to the project. But if you don't want to settle for the images in the Cricut Image Library images, you can create your own images, upload, and cut them using your Cricut machine.

If you are using a Mac or Windows PC, open the Design Space, sign in with your Cricut ID and password, click on "Images," and browse, search, or filter the images you need to design your project.

'Images' option on Canvas

Crafters using iOS or Android are not left out. Run the process by tapping on the "Image" button on your iOS and Android app. Here's what you get to see when you launch the process via your PC, iOS, and Android device.

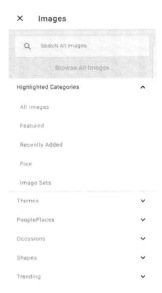

Highlighted image categories

- All Images: Use this option to search for specific images from the Cricut Image Library.
- Categories: Click this option and select the category that suits your project to see a pool of relevant images.
- Cartridges: A click on this option will pop up over 400 Cricut cartridges, and carefully search for the right one(s) for your project.

BROWSE AND SEARCH FOR CARTRIDGES

Cartridges come with designs you can use to create lovely projects. Images within these cartridges share similar design styles, and they can add striking effects to your Cricut projects. You can easily browse and search for your favorite cartridges on the internet. How? Just follow these simple steps to browse and search for your favorite cartridges.

Step 1. Launch Cricut on your PC > use your ID and password to log in to your account.

USING IMAGES IN DESIGN SPACE | 153

Cricut Sign in page

Step 2. Access the Cricut Image library > navigate your Design Panel to locate the Image Tab > click the tab to open a window that houses the Image Library.

Cricut image library

Step 3. Tap the Cartridges tab to open an alphabetical list of many cartridges, including all Cricut cartridges. Each cartridge comes with a horizontal tile.

Each cartridge tile has the name and the image samples of the cartridge it represents. Check the right view of each cartridge to see the number of images they have and how to access them. While some of these cartridges are free of charge, you have to purchase or subscribe for others before you can access them.

The cartridges are displayed alphabetically. If you don't want to scroll through in that order, you can filter by cartridge category or simply search for a particular cartridge. How can I search for a particular cartridge? No worries. Click on the search field > type the cartridge name > tap on your magnifying glass to open the cartridge.

154 | BOOK 2

Using the image search field

Step 4. Click on "View All Images" if you want to see all the images in a given cartridge. The "View All Images" button lies close to the Cartridge Tile, on its right side.

As soon as you click the "View All Images" button, the images on the selected cartridge will be displayed, and you can simply search or filter the image you need to create your Cricut project.

Filtering Cricut image categories

Step 5. Select your favorite image and click on "Insert Images" to upload the image on your Canvas.

SEARCH FOR CARTRIDGES WITH A FILTER

Designs from cartridges may be used to create beautiful Cricut projects. You already know that images within cartridges come with similar design styles, and they can spice up your Cricut projects. Here, I will show you how you can easily search for cartridges with a filter. Just follow these simple steps to access cartridges with a filter.

Step 1. Navigate the Cricut Image Library to access all sorts of cartridge options. How? Locate the Design Panel and click on the Images Tab to pop up a window that houses the Image Library.

USING IMAGES IN DESIGN SPACE | 155

Cricut image library

Step 2. Tap the Cartridges Tab to pop up over 400 cartridges. These cartridges are alphabetically listed. Each Cricut cartridge comes with a horizontal tile.

Cricut cartridges' tab

The tile has the name and image samples of the cartridge it represents. Each cartridge has its specified number of images, well displayed on its right side, as well as its access plans. If access is not free, you may have to purchase or subscribe for a cartridge before you can use it.

Feel free to scroll through the alphabetical list of cartridges on display. You may also search for a particular cartridge or filter by cartridge category. How can I get to see the available filters for the cartridge category? Go to the top-right-hand corner of your screen and tap the "Filters Menu."

156 | BOOK 2

Images on the filters menu

Step 3. Choose the filter you want to use for the cartridge view. Click on "Apply."

Here are a few options for cartridge filters. Take your time to consider their level of access.

- My Cartridges: You get to see free, purchased, and linked cartridges here, including Cricut Access.

1. Free: You can use cartridges here free of charge.
2. Purchased: You get to see the digital cartridges you purchased and those that were linked to your Cricut machine.
3. Cricut Access: Membership is required to use Cricut Access. Remember we discussed this extensively in Chapter One. You can run through the chapter again to know how you can use the platform.

Step 4. Click on "View All Images" to pop up the images on a selected cartridge. Search and filter the image you need to create your Cricut project.

Cricut image' samples

Step 5. Select the image > tap "Insert Images" button > add the image to your Canvas.

USING IMAGES IN DESIGN SPACE | 157

DOWNLOAD CRICUT CARTRIDGE ONLINE

Cricut cartridge is available for download online. Freely download your favorite cartridge online to create your adorable Cricut project. To make the download, ready your Cricut Expression, Cricut USB cable, Cricut Design Studio software, PC, and stable internet connection. Stay tuned as David Cavalier (N. D.) takes us through the process of downloading Cricut Cartridge from the internet. Just follow these simple steps to download your own Cricut cartridge.

Step 1. Run the Design studio software on your computer and follow the instructions that pop up to download the cartridge.

Step 2. Reboot your PC once the program has been successfully installed.

Step 3. Use the USB plugin for your Cricut studio kit to connect your Cricut Expression to the computer.

Step 4. Switch on the Cricut Expression machine and check whether your computer could recognize it.

Step 5. Feed a Cricut cartridge into your Expression machine. No worries if the cartridge is not the one you want to cut from.

Step 6. Use the various file-sharing sites to download your favorite Cricut cartridges.

Step 7. Launch your Cricut Design studio program > download the images or cartridges you want > arrange and cut your design with the Design studio program > click on the "Cut" button as soon as you complete the design.

You just learned how to download your Cricut cartridge from the internet. Still, don't be in a hurry to download from any file-sharing sites you come across on the internet. Why? Some of these sites have corrupt files, and they can damage your computer. Share your cartridges with known people or trusted sources.

How can I see the cartridges that are linked to my Cricut account? No worries. Use your Cricut ID and password to sign in on cricut.com > tap the person icon > select My Account > navigate the menu and click on Linked Cartridges.

PURCHASING IMAGES ON CRICUT DESIGN SPACE

Lots of images are available for purchase via the Cricut Image Library. You can access the images using your Mac or Windows PC and iOS or Android device. Ready? Select the option that works for you and follow the attached steps.

It is relatively easy to purchase images via Cricut Design Space using your computer or mobile. But before you launch the process, click on the Design Space menu, and select your region. Currently, only residents in Canada, Australia, the UK, and the US can purchase images via the platform.

MAC OR WINDOWS PC

Here is how you can easily purchase images with your PC.

158 | BOOK 2

Step 1. Add the image or images to your design > click the Edit bar to open a drop-down menu > select the image you want to purchase

Selecting an image to purchase via Cricut access

Step 2. Click on Make It > review the images you want to purchase > supply your payment information.

Reviewing the selected image before purchase is made

Step 3. Add your Cricut password to authorize the purchase.

USING IMAGES IN DESIGN SPACE | 159

Payment information for Cricut access image purchase

No issues if you don't want to add an image to your project before you could purchase it. You can always do it your way. Just click the Information icon > Buy Image > supply your payment information > authorize the purchase by entering your Cricut password.

IOS

Just follow these simple steps to purchase images via your iOS device.

Step 1. Use your Cricut ID and password to sign in to Design Space > launch a new project > navigate the bottom-left corner of the screen to select your image.

Step 2. Click on Cartridges > locate the image you want to purchase > tap the Buy this Cartridge option.

Step 3. Review the list of images > click on Continue > select Purchase

Step 4. Sign in with your Apple ID and password to authorize the purchase.

You can make your in-app purchases via your iTunes account. You'll get the summary of your order from the App Store as soon as you complete the purchase.

ANDROID DEVICE

Simply follow these simple steps to purchase images via your Android device.

Step 1. Open your project > navigate the Edit tool to pop up a drop-down menu > add the image you want to purchase to your project.

A Cricut image to purchase

Step 2. Click on Make It > tap Purchase option > review the images you want to purchase > tap the Continue button.

USING IMAGES IN DESIGN SPACE | 161

Reviewing an image before purchase is made

Step 3. Click on Buy > supply your Google Play password > authorize the purchase by tapping Verify.

Use your Google Play account to make your Android in-app purchases. As soon as you complete the order, you will get the summary of the order in your Google Play store account. Navigate the "Purchased or My Images filter" to see the purchased content.

UPLOADING IMAGES INTO DESIGN SPACE

Feel free to upload your images through Cricut Design Space. Also, apart from uploading the images free of charge, you can convert the images to cuttable shapes via the software. But, before we look at how to upload your pictures through your PC and iOS or Android device, let's quickly look at Basic and Vector—the two forms of uploaded images.

Basic or Raster Images

Images in .jpeg, .png, .gif, and .bmp files are Basic images. Upload these images as single layers, and feel free to edit them while they are being uploaded.

Vector Images

Images in .svg, and .dxf files are Vector images. You can upload these images the way they were previously designed. As soon as you upload and save the image files, they automatically separate into different layers.

Cricut images can be uploaded with computers running on Mac or Windows, iOS, and Android devices.

How to Upload Images with Your:

PC

Follow these simple steps to upload your Cricut images through your computer.

Step 1. Launch your Cricut > use your ID and password to log in to your account > navigate the left side of the Canvas to click on Upload > select "Image" or "Pattern" upload. (You will select Image here because we are not dealing with patterns). With the Upload Image option, you can work with .gif, .png, .bmp, .jpg, and other basic image files, as well as .svg and .dxf image files.

Design Space upload page

Step 2. Click on Upload Image to open a drop-down menu > select Browse to pop up the file selector > navigate to the image you want to use > drag or drop the image file in the Upload window.

Drag or drop page for uploading Cricut images

USING IMAGES IN DESIGN SPACE | 163

Browsing for desired image to upload

Be prepared to run through the Basic image upload process if you intend to upload .jpg, .png, .gif, .bmp, or any other Basic image files. But, should you choose .svg or .dxf image file, you'll have to run the upload process via the Vector image upload channel.

Basic Image Upload

- Click on the .png, .bmp, .gif, or .jpg image you intend to upload > navigate the file selector to click on Open, or simply drag and drop the image to the image upload window in the Design Space.

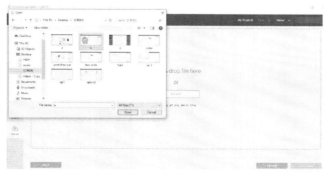

Uploading an image into Design Space Canvas

- Use the descriptions on your screen to rate the image as Simple, Moderately Complex, or Complex, depending on the image you intend to upload > click on Continue.

164 | BOOK 2

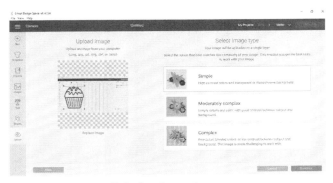

Design Space image rating page

- Use Erase, Select Erase, and Crop tools to edit the image and clean the unwanted areas within the image, including its background.

Select and erase page for uploaded image

- As soon as you remove the unwanted areas, click on Preview to see the cut lines around your image. Should you have issues viewing the image the way you want, click the Editing view > remove the part you don't want to see in the image > click on Continue once you are satisfied with the image.
- Create a name for the uploaded image.

USING IMAGES IN DESIGN SPACE | 165

Saving an image on Design Space

Would you like to tag the image so that everyone can easily locate it online? It's fine if you want to. Still, make up your mind to either save the image as a "Cut" or "Print Then Cut" image. It all depends on what you want.

Just know that if the image is saved as a "Print Then Cut" image, the entire image will be secured, including the patterns and internal colors. You only get to save the outer silhouette of the uploaded image if you opt for the "Cut" image option.

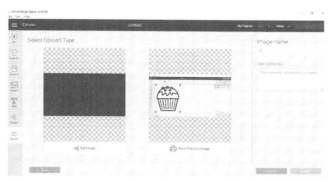

Design Space options for saving Cricut images

- Click on Save as soon as you are done.

The program will take you back to the Upload screen, and you get to see the uploaded image in the Uploaded Images Library. Navigate the bottom part of the screen to locate the library.

How can I add the uploaded image to my project? No worries. Select the image and tap the Insert Image icon. It's that simple.

Inserting Cricut images into the Canvas

Vector Image Upload

- Click on the .dxf or .svg image file you intend to upload > navigate the file selector to tap the Open button > drag and move the image to the Image upload window.

Image files designed on other software will work fine on Design Space. Feel free to use a solid color, solid color fills, outlined layers, and other beautiful images on your Design Space. Still, should you use a layered image, make sure that you ungroup the layers in the original file.

- Create a name for the uploaded image > tag the image to make it accessible for people online > click on Save.

The program will take you back to the Upload screen, and the uploaded image will be listed in the uploaded photo, right there in the Uploaded Images Library. Select the image and tap Insert Images to move the uploaded image to your design screen.

IOS

Just follow these simple steps to upload your images via your iOS device.

Step 1. Launch your Design Space > use your Cricut ID and password to log in to your account > navigate the bottom toolbar to click on the Upload tool.

USING IMAGES IN DESIGN SPACE | 167

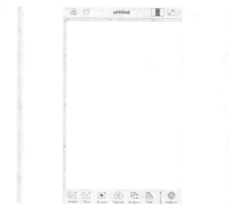

Design Space on iOS. Photo via Holli Mostella

Step 2. Choose an image. You can open uploaded images, browse files, or simply use your Camera Roll to get an image.

Preparing to upload an image. Photo via Holli Mostella

Step 3. Choose "Browse files" if you want to select iCloud, Dropbox, Google Drive, or other file storage applications on your device. Just select the location of the image file to browse the image. However, how this runs depends on the version of iOS you have on your device.

Don't worry if you have uploaded a vector image. The vector image already has a defined cut path, and it will be automatically saved in your Uploaded Images library.

Step 4. Create a name for the uploaded image > navigate the upper right corner of your screen to find the Save button > click on Save. The Uploaded Images library should open as soon as you save the image. Should you need to work with a picture in your project, select and insert one from the library.

168 | BOOK 2

Saving an uploaded image. Photo via Holli Mostella

You'll get a basic image like GIF, BMP, JPG, or PNG if you took a picture with the camera of your iOS device or simply selected a photo via your Camera Roll. Should this be the case, get ready to clean the image. Why do I need to clean up the image? You need it because you have to remove the unwanted areas of the image and also define its cut lines. Here are the available clean-up tools in Cricut Design Space.

Remove, erase, crop options. Photo via Lorrie Nunemaker

Remove

A click on this tool will remove the connected areas with the same color. How can I use the Remove tool? Click and hold the area you want to remove > zoom in on the area to see it very clearly > increase or decrease the tool's capacity, using a slider.

USING IMAGES IN DESIGN SPACE | 169

Removing the unwanted areas in an image. Photo via Lorrie Nunemaker

Use the checkered background to know the area to remove from the image.

Check the upper-right part of the image. Do you see a cut preview? It should appear while you're cleaning the image. Click on the preview to minimize or enlarge the image.

Erase

Click the Erase tool to clean the areas of an image. How? Place a finger on the part or area of the image to remove > increase or decrease the eraser's dimension, using a slider > zoom in on the area to see the image more clearly.

Erasing some portions in an image. Photo via Lorrie Nunemaker

Crop

Use this tool to shape your image and trim its edges. Just tap on the tool > drag its handles from the four corners of the image > click on Done to crop the covered area.

Using the crop tool on an image. Photo via Lorrie Nunemaker

Should there be a mistake during the cropping process or you want to reset the image, click on the circular arrow close to the center bottom of your screen. Navigate the upper-right corner of the screen to click on Next as soon as you finish cleaning the image.

Refine Screen

Use the refine tool to add final touches to the image before saving it in the Cricut Image Library.

An image on the refine screen. Photo via Cricut

Click on the image preview to opt for a cut or print view. Use these tools to refine your image.

- **Despeckle:** Use this tool to quickly clean small artifacts from the image. But if you're dealing with larger artifacts, move the slider to the right a bit to rove the artifacts.

A despeckled image. Photo via Cricut

- **Smooth:** Use this tool to simplify the jagged lines of your image. How? Highlight the

USING IMAGES IN DESIGN SPACE | 171

image and click on Smooth. Don't hesitate to use the tool as many times as you want. Tap Reset if you want to start the process all over.

A smoothened image. Photo via Cricut. Cricut houses vital tips to mastering the Design Space.

Step 5. Click on Next as soon as you finish the refining process.

Step 6. Create a name for the image > choose how you want to save the image (Print Them Cut or Cut Image) > click Save.

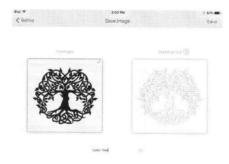

Saving the image. Photo via Cricut. Vital tips on how to use Design Space effortlessly are available on Cricut.

ANDROID DEVICE

Follow these simple steps to use your Android device to upload your own Cricut images.

Step 1. Navigate the bottom toolbar > click on the Upload tool > choose your upload option (use your uploaded images, pick an image from the Images library, or use your camera to take an image).

172 | BOOK 2

Design Space Image upload option for Android device

Step 2. Click on "Select from Photo Library" to use an image from Google Drive, OneDrive, Dropbox, or other file storage applications on your Android device > choose the location of the image file > click on "Next" to browse and locate the image. How the process runs on your device depends on the version of Android you are using.

Uploading an image via Design Space

Step 3. Create a name for the image and click on Save.

USING IMAGES IN DESIGN SPACE | 173

Saving option for Cricut images

The Uploaded Images library should open once you save the image. Click on the library to select and insert a picture in your project. You can also access the uploaded images through your Images screen. Use the tag or name of an uploaded image to locate the image via the Images screen.

USE THE SLICE TOOL TO EDIT YOUR CRICUT IMAGES

You can edit your images with the Slice tool. It is simple, easy, and convenient, and I will be showing you how to do it. Causey (2018) knows the steps to take to edit your Cricut images with the Slice tool.

Step 1. Launch your Cricut Design Space to open your Canvas > click on the image you want to upload > tap Insert. Just make sure your image is big enough, or you will have issues working on it.

Design Space page for image insert

Step 2. Click the right-bottom corner of the Canvas > drag it down a little > navigate the left side of the toolbox > click on the Shape > click the Square.

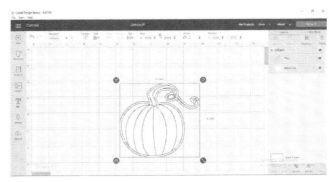

Design Space page for adding a shape on the Canvas

Step 3. Click the small circle under the Square to unlock the Square > use the small circle to adjust the shape of the Square as you want.

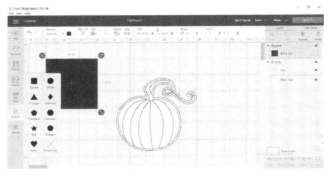

Adding a desired shape to the Canvas

Step 4. Click or highlight the Square > tap and hold the Shift button on your keyboard > use the Mouse to left-click the bubble image.

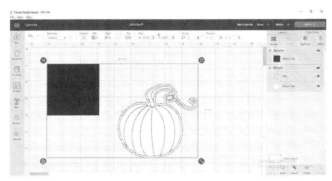

Highlighting the shape and uploaded image

USING IMAGES IN DESIGN SPACE | 175

Step 5. Navigate the bottom-right corner of your Canvas to click on the Slice tool > pull the pieces of the slice away > delete the pieces.

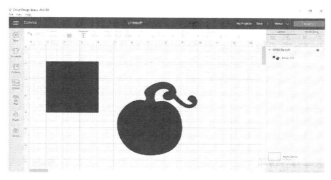

Using the slice tool to separate the images

You just learned how to use the Slice tool to edit your images. Feel free to start the process all over again until the edited image looks right for you.

EDIT YOUR IMAGES IN UPLOAD MODE

Freely edit your images on the Cricut Design Space while you are getting the images uploaded. Currently, you can only use your PC to edit images in upload mode, not your iOS or Android device. Follow these simple steps to do it.

Step 1. Upload an image and click on Complex to pop up the next window.

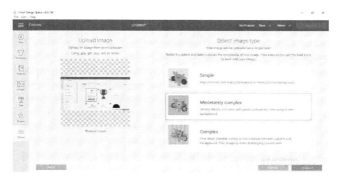

Design Space upload page

Step 2. Navigate the Wand tool through the top-left hand corner of Design Space

Inserting the image to edit on Design Space

Step 3. Click on Magic Wand > tap Continue > rename the image > click Save.

Saving the image on the canvas

You just learned how to edit your images in Upload mode. Open your Cricut Design Space, try what you've just learned, and you will see how easy it is.

CREATE LAYERS AND SEPARATE OBJECTS

You can create layers and separate objects via your Design Space. Here, I will teach you how to do it, but first things first: Let's see how to create layers.

Create Cricut Layers

Follow these simple steps to create and cut your Cricut layers.

Step 1. Launch your Cricut Design Space > tap the Upload Image icon > upload the image you want to use to create the layers > select the Moderately Complex button > click on Continue.

USING IMAGES IN DESIGN SPACE | 177

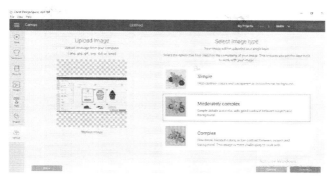

Design Space upload page

Step 2. Click on the areas you want to remove in the image, including the background > use the Magic Wand tool to delete the unwanted areas > cut the image to form the base of the layers.

Deleting the unwanted areas in the uploaded image

Step 3. Click on Preview to run a preview screen check on the image > click on Continue if you love the silhouette of the image > select "Save as a cut file" or "Save as a print and cut file" option.

178 | BOOK 2

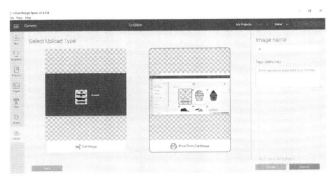

Creating image name to save the Cricut image

Step 4. Navigate to Upload Image > upload the image again > tap on Moderately Complex button > click on Continue.

Step 5. Remove unwanted areas and the background again with the Magic Wand > do away with all colors in the image, except one, to create the first layer > click on Continue > Select "Save the image as a cut file" option.

Adding additional layers to a Cricut design

Step 6. Add the layers to your Designs Space > click on the "Make It" icon.

Separate Your Images from a Multiple Image

Just follow these simple steps to separate your images from multiple images.

Step 1. Launch your Cricut Design Space > navigate the Left toolbar > tap the Upload Image icon > click on Upload.

USING IMAGES IN DESIGN SPACE | 179

Design Space upload page

Step 2. Click on Moderately Complex button > tap Continue > select the crop tool > crop the image you want to separate from the multiple images.

'Moderately Complex' option on Design Space

Step 3. Tap the Magic wand tool > click the areas you don't want around the selected image, including the background > click on preview to remove the areas you don't want > tap Continue.

Previewing the uploaded image

Step 4. Click on the Print and Cut option > rename the image > click on Save. Repeat the process to separate other images on the multiple images.

Renaming the image in order to save it

Step 5. Select the separated images > insert them on your Cricut Design Space.

Saving the project

You just successfully separated the images on the Design Space screen. Feel free to resize the images and click on "Make It" to print and Cut the image.

Learning how to use images in Cricut Design Space is another giant stride in your determination to become a pro in Cricut designs, and you're surely getting there soon. Next, I will walk you through "Useful Tips in Advanced Design Space," our focus for the next chapter. Eager to see you there!

5

USEFUL TIPS IN ADVANCED DESIGN SPACE

Cricut machines can cut all sorts of materials, and you need to master how it works. How to master the machine has generated little or no concern in the last few years. The main concerns relate to Cricut software, the Design Space. Cricut Design Space is relatively easy to use and master, but some of its tools and features do not take the regular structure most of us had expected. And, for a newbie, mastering Cricut Design Space could be overly complicated, despite its basic and simple techniques. But once you start rolling out a few projects, you will find that the software has all you need to design adorable Cricut projects. The Design Space lets you access wonderful shortcuts to make your crafting easy and efficient.

Still, many crafters, including the intermediate ones, underutilize the software because they barely understand what each icon or panel on the Design Space Canvas Area stands for. Fine, we already dealt with that in Chapter Two. Yet, your desire to create unique Cricut projects with absolute ease and confidence should know no bounds. For this reason, I will share useful tips and tricks in Advance Design Space with you, and you won't have any issues crafting your favorite project.

DESIGN CANVAS TIPS

Design Canvas allows you to create, edit, and manipulate your designs. Virtually all the fantastic things you do on the Cricut software occur within the Design Canvas Area. Remember I took you through the Canvas Area in Chapter Two, and here you get to see several wonderful Design Canvas tips to make your next Cricut project unique, efficient, and convenient. Just make sure nothing shifts your focus while I walk you through the tips, one after the other.

1. Use Slice, Contour, and Weld to Customize Your Designs: Feel free to change, personalize, or customize the images you upload from your personal files or the Design Space Image Library. Slice, Contour, and Weld are the three editing tools to use to carry out this function. How can I locate these editing tools? No issues. Just check the right side of the bottom toolbar.

182 | BOOK 2

However, the functions aren't available all the time. But once you have a design that is compatible with the functions, the tools will pop up. These tools might look insignificant at first glance, but you can't personalize your designs without them.

The Slice Tool

Click on the Slice tool to split two overlapping text or images to separate parts or create several new shapes from the overlapped images or text.

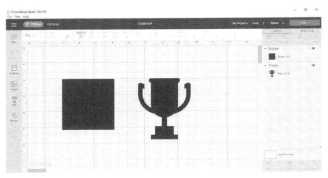

An uploaded image and shape

The new shapes will still appear separately in the Layers panel, although you are free to keep or discard them. Here are tips on how to use the Slice tool effortlessly and efficiently.

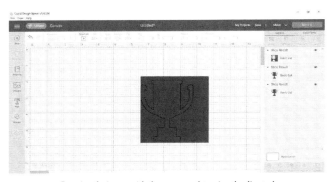

Covering the image with the square and tapping the slice tool

- Focus on two layers at a time when using Slice with images.
- Ungroup or hide other layers in a multi-layered image to activate the Slice tool.
- Hidden layers are removed from the Layers panel or design screen when you run the Slice function on hidden layers. Still, you can use images on the hidden layers in your project. How? Ungroup the layers before you start using the Slice tool.

USEFUL TIPS IN ADVANCED DESIGN SPACE | 183

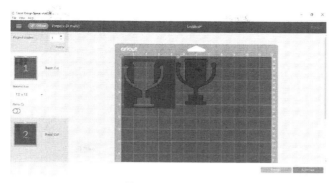

The already sliced image

The Weld Tool

Click on the Weld tool to join different shapes to design a customized image or remove overlapped cut lines. Use the tool to simplify your design, connect the text, and combine shapes to create striking aesthetic effects. Here are tips on how to use the Weld tool effortlessly and efficiently.

- Overlap the text and images to weld.

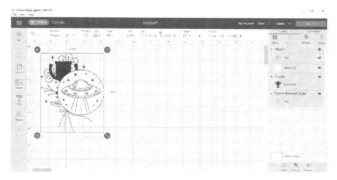

A set of overlapped images

- Ungroup each layer in your multi-layered images and make sure they are individually arranged before you start the welding process.

184 | BOOK 2

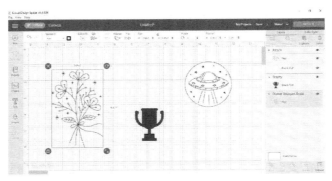

The overlapped images now ungrouped

- Select one or more layers to activate the weld tool.

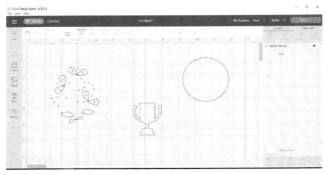

Activating the weld tool by selecting layers of the image

- Welded images turn to the same color while the new image pops up in the Layers panel as soon as you complete the welding process.

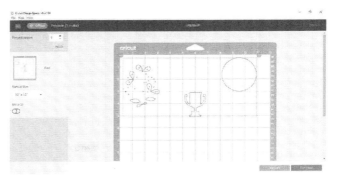

A set of welded images

- Watch the new layer appear at the top of the Layers panel. But, should it not be so, arrange or drag the new layer to the Layers panel.

Using Contour Function in Design Space

Use the Contour tool to hide parts of an image layer or remove unwanted cut lines. Just follow these simple steps to use the Contour function in Cricut Design Space.

Step 1. Ungroup the image. If your image has multiple layers, carefully ungroup the image. How you run this function depends on the device you're using.

Crafters with Mac or Windows Desktop should select the image and click on Ungroup (located at the upper part of the Layers panel). Users of iOS and Android can also run this function via their device. Just select the image and navigate to the "Actions menu" to click on the "Ungroup" button.

Step 2. Select the layer that houses the cut lines you want to hide. To do this, click on "Contour" in your Layers panel if you are using Windows or Mac Desktop. Android or iOS users should simply navigate the Actions menu to select "Hide Contour."

Step 3. Select the contour to hide. Watch out for the separate cut lines on the selected image if you are using a Mac or Windows PC, and click the cut line of the image you intend to hide. If this option does not work for you, navigate the menu via the right side of the window to click on the contour button. Watch as the hidden contour turns to a lighter shade. With this, be rest assured that the hidden contour ceases to be a part of the designed image.

The process is a little different for iOS and Android users. Images on iOS and Android come with cut lines, represented by dark gray lines. Just click the corresponding dark gray line to hide a particular image. Once done, the line will turn light gray.

Step 4. Close the "Hide Contour" window as soon as you hide the desired cut lines.

2. Do Some Search Terms' Experiment: Use the Design Space Image Library search function to access and get amazing images for your project. Vary your search words to pop up a significant amount of images. Change a character or a single letter in your search words and see how many images pop up on your screen. Do you understand how this works? Play with words and do lots of searches to get the exact images for your project. Using synonyms to search for images is another great option. How does this help? People tag images with different terms, remember.

Searching Cricut images via Design Space

So, if you use synonyms, you'll have several image options to choose from. For example, if you need cut labels, possible images will pop up when you use search words such as label, circle, tag, rectangle, and square. Still, with garden, spring, flower, plant, heart, love, Valentine, or similar words, you get unique images for your project, although this depends on the nature of the project being designed.

3. Check for More Images from a Chosen Cartridge: At times, after a search, you only love one image out of the whole variety, and you ask yourself what you can do to get more photos like the current one. No issues. Check the cartridge that houses the image you already have. Yes, the one you love. How do I access the cartridge? Each image in the Design Space Image Library comes with a small "(i)."

Retrieving images from specific cartridges

Check the bottom right-hand corner of the image you love and click the "(i)" to access a full set of the images.

4. Use Free Text and Images: It is fine if you are not a fan of Cricut Access or you don't have the money to opt for any of its subscription plans. You can still up your crafting skills by utilizing the free text and images in the Cricut Design Space. The free resources are rich and appealing. How do I get these free text and images? Simply tap the Filter in the Design Space Image Library to access the "Free" option to open the free text and images.

USEFUL TIPS IN ADVANCED DESIGN SPACE | 187

Finding free text and images via Design Space

Select and insert the ones you need into your design.

5. Do Quick Re-Coloring: Use the Color Sync tool to quickly embellish your project with your favorite color. With this tool, you can select the same colors for all the designs within your project. For example, rather than coloring the design one layer at a time, use the Color Sync tool to create various shades of your favorite colors on your design.

Your project will display the available colors. Still, feel free to drag a layer of your design on a color you deem fit or perfect for the layer. Decide whether to use a single color consistently throughout the design or to vary the layers' color.

Design Space quick recoloring page

However, to achieve efficient, easy, and quick cutting, opt for the Color Sync tool.

6. Use the Hide Tool: You are likely to insert too many images when working on a project. But, most times, you end up not cutting all these images on your canvas. Yet, you don't have to delete your canvas just because you won't be cutting all the images. Simply click the "hide" option to avoid cutting the left-out images. The hide option looks like an eye, and each image has it. Simply navigate the right-hand Layers to use the hide tool.

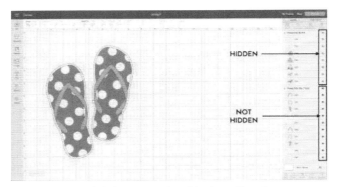

Using the hide too to customize a Cricut image. Photo via TheHomesIHaveMade

A click on the hide tool will remove the unwanted image from the canvas. And, when you finally cut the project, hidden images won't be included.

7. Change Lines to Draw, Score, or Cut: At one time, crafters had to opt for a design with the line's attributes they wanted to score or draw.

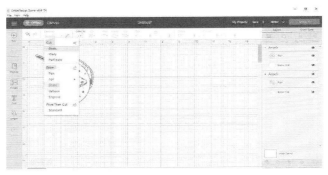

Draw, score, and cut line options on Design Space

Now, due to Design Space's improvement, you can draw any line and simply change the line to cut or score via the Line type drop-down menu. Designs on your canvas will appear as "Cut" designs but feel free to use pens to draw your image outlines, just as the scoring tool or scoring wheel could be used to score your images.

8. Manipulate Patterns: Use the Fill tool to manipulate how you fill the image in your design. Do you know where to find the Fill tool? It lies around the top toolbar. Get ready to swap colors or assign patterns to each image in the design as soon as you select a layer. Using preloaded patterns to fill images in your design is fun, and you don't have to use cardstock or patterned scrapbook paper to manipulate the images in your Cricut project.

USEFUL TIPS IN ADVANCED DESIGN SPACE | 189

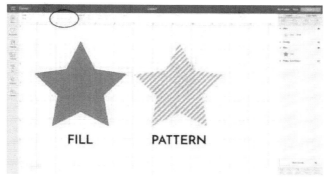

Manipulative patterns. Photo via TheHomesIHaveMade

Lots of design options await you when you manipulate your Cricut patterns. Still, you can take a step further by manipulating the orientation and scale of your pattern. How? Navigate the Pattern menu and click on Edit Pattern.

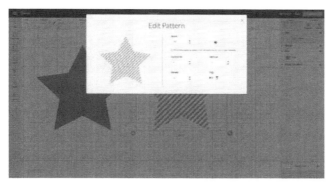

Editing the manipulative pattern. Photo via TheHomesIHaveMade

The pattern option won't work unless you use the Print-then-Cut technique.

9. Utilize Keyboard Shortcuts: Design Space canvas comes with Duplicate, Delete, Copy, Cut, Paste, and other useful commands. Check the right-hand Layers Panel, the top toolbar, and the edges of your images to see these command buttons. Utilize the keyboard shortcuts of your PC to run desired commands. Simply use "Control C" to copy a file, "Control V" to paste the file, and "Control Z" for Undo. Using shortcuts to run your designs means that you'll save lots of time perfecting a Cricut project.

10. Utilize Slice to Crop: Cricut Design Space does not have the Crop tool. Still, you can quickly and easily slice your designs or shave off unwanted parts from your designs. How? Use the Slice tool and free shapes, like circle or square) to crop your designs. Sure, it may not be as easy as using the regular Crop tool, but you can master it.

190 | BOOK 2

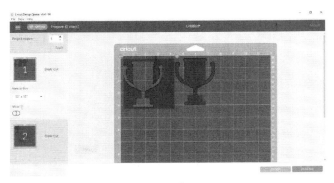

A well cropped image

Navigate to the left panel of your canvas > click on Upload > select the image to crop > add your favorite shape for cropping > overlap the shape on the image to crop > select the image and the shape > click on the Slice tool.

CUT SCREEN TIPS

Cut Screen relates to the series of screens that pop up when you click on "Make It" to set the cut settings for your Cricut projects. Your control over your project does not end after you finish the project or cut the images with a click on the "Make It" button. No! You can manipulate the cut screen to save lots of materials and time. How? Pay keen attention to these Cut Screen tips to make your next project easy, convenient, and efficient.

1. Drag Items about the Mat: Use the items to encircle the mat within the cut screen. True, the Design Space can auto-populate the images on the mats with desired color and orientation. Still, the images may not be in the intended locations. How can I work this out? Drag and drop the images on the mat and use the handles to rotate the mat. This way, you can move your images to the favored location.

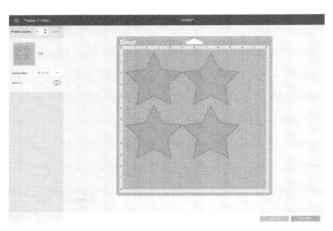

Images dragged around the Cricut mat. Photo via TheHomesIHaveMade

USEFUL TIPS IN ADVANCED DESIGN SPACE | 191

Make sure that the color of the gridlines on your mat matches that of the screen, or your design and material won't look good.

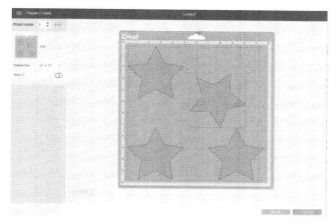

Rotated images. Photo via TheHomesIHaveMade

2. Budge Images across Mat: Don't just budge your images around the mat. No. Freely move each image from one mat to the other. Yes, you don't need to change your images' color via design canvas simply because you're moving them across the mat. How can I budge my images from one mat to another? No worries. Here is how.

- Navigate the upper left-hand corner of the image you want to move.

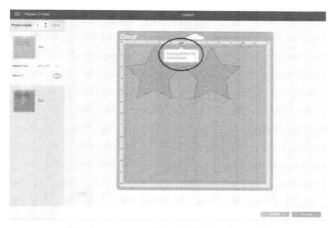

Cricut images on a mat. Photo via TheHomesIHaveMade

- Click on the three (3) dots to open a drop-down menu.

192 | BOOK 2

Preparing to budge the images across mat. Photo via TheHomesIHaveMade

- Click on the "Move to another mat" option.

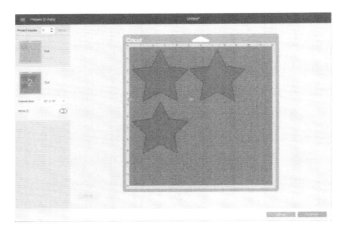

Moving the images to another mat. Photo via TheHomesIHaveMade

Design Space will ask you to choose the mat that will house the images.

3. Combining Cricut Projects on One Window: There was a time when users of Cricut Design Space couldn't combine two or more projects in one window. But thanks to Cricut upgrading their services, the whole process has changed. So, as it stands, you can combine several Cricut projects when you're working on Design Space.

Still, make sure you update your Design Space to the latest version (6.0.150) if you want to enjoy this feature. Visit design.cricut.com to update your Cricut Design Space.

Only then can you start to combine your projects. How? Just follow these simple steps.

USEFUL TIPS IN ADVANCED DESIGN SPACE | 193

Step 1. Launch your Cricut Design Space on your PC > click open a project > minimize the window.

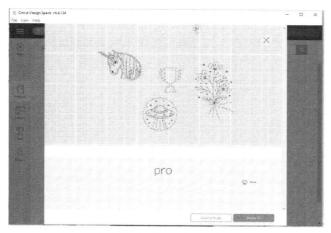

A minimized project window on Canvas

Step 2. Tap File > New Window > View all your projects > select the project to combine with the one in the minimized window > click on Customize > highlight the portion to combine (if you're not planning to copy the whole project) > right-click on the portion and choose Copy.

Copying a set of images on another project window

Step 3. Open the minimized window > right-click > choose Paste.

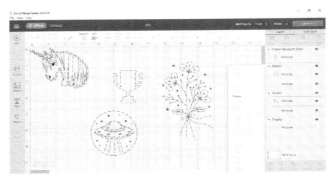

Pasting the copied images into the previous project window

You get to see both projects on one window. If you want to add another project, just repeat the process.

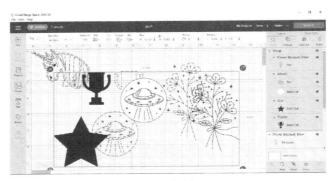

A combination of all the images

4. Save the Cut Materials You Always Use: Don't discard your preferred cut materials. There are chances you will soon need the materials to create another project.

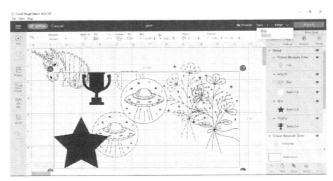

Using the 'save' option to save your cut materials

Navigate the Cricut Design Space to locate the Custom Materials menu. Click the menu and follow the pop-up instructions to save those materials.

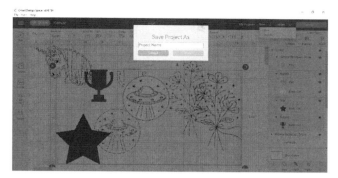

'Save project as' page on the Canvas

5. Skip and Repeat Mats: Design Space makes crafting effortless and convenient. You have nothing to worry about once you click the "Make It" option and your design is sent to cut, provided the right paper and color are fed into the Cricut machine. Your project will come out clean and clearly cut! Still, you can skip or repeat mats as you want. What does this mean? You can decide the mat to cut next, the one to re-cut, and the mat to skip without leaving the cut screen.

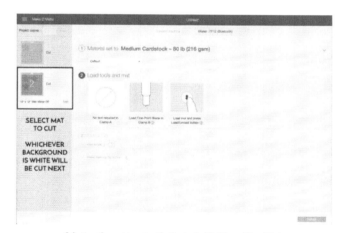

Selecting the mat to cut with. Photo via TheHomesIHaveMade

Just select the mat to cut next before you feed your mat into the Cricut machine. How? Highlight the mat > click its left-hand side > select your favorite option.

6. Connect Several Cricut Machines at Once: It is fine if you don't have more than one Cricut machine. But if you have two, feel free to combine them to your Design Space account at a go. Yes, use Bluetooth or USB to launch the connection. What if I used the wrong machine to cut a project? No worries. The software will ask you to confirm the machine you want to work

with via its final cut screen. The issue of creating a wrong design with the wrong machine will never come up.

7. Edit Cut Setting for all Your Materials: Set your Cricut machine to Vinyl when cutting your materials. The machine might not cut through all the materials but no worries. Feel free to adjust your Cricut machine's settings to set its depth, blade, and how often the machine will make passes. Just click the Materials menu to make the changes. How?

- Click on the Materials menu on the Cut Screen > select "Materials" if you are not using Cricut Maker > set the machine dial to "Custom."

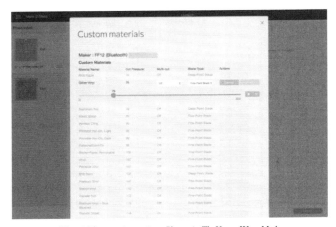

Materials' cut setting options. Photo via TheHomesIHaveMade

- Click on Browse All Materials > tap Material Settings > select any material and adjust its settings.

8. Adjust Your Cut Pressure: Were you able to edit the Cut setting for your materials? Awesome! You don't need to make much effort to run the process; you just have to adjust your cut pressure to neatly cut through the materials.

USEFUL TIPS IN ADVANCED DESIGN SPACE | 197

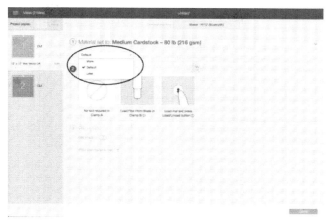

Adjusting cut pressure for Design Space projects. Photo via TheHomesIHaveMade

How can I do it? Click on the Materials menu > Browse All Materials to open a drop-down menu > change the pressure to Default.

9. Change Project Copies to Fill Mat: The Cricut "Autofill" feature is not available anymore. Before, you could select your paper size, create a star or other customized designs on your canvas, click the feature, and comfortably fill up the paper with the customized designs. Great, wasn't it? "Autofill" is unavailable on Design Space, but you still can fill your mat with your beautiful project copies. How?

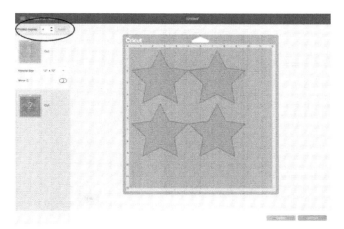

Changing project copies to fill mat. Photo via TheHomesIHaveMade

Navigate your first cut screen for the "Project Copies" option. Use this function to cut the content of your design canvas as you want.

Getting to know the number of copies you need to cover the mat may require a trial-and-error approach. Still, it is the best alternative to looking for duplicates on the canvas to fill the mat.

10. Position Mirror on the Cut Screen: Iron-On projects, like some other projects, demand special attention. You may have to reverse the cutting pattern of your designs when you work on such projects. A reversed design cut is also known as "Mirror." Sure, you can flip your design horizontally on your design canvas, but that's going to take you lots of time. Use the "Mirror your designs" option on the cut screen.

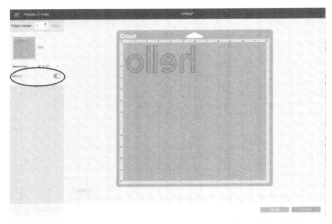

'Mirror your Designs' option on cut screen. Photo via TheHomesIHaveMade

A click on the "Mirror your designs" option will walk you through a simple process where you will create, tweak, and customize your design easily on the cut screen.

11. Pay Keen Attention to Instructions: Get used to Design Space invaluable reminders if you want your projects to turn out great. For example, the Cricut software will remind you to Mirror your designs when you click on "Iron-On." You will also be told to lay the vinyl's shiny part on the cutting mat.

USEFUL TIPS IN ADVANCED DESIGN SPACE | 199

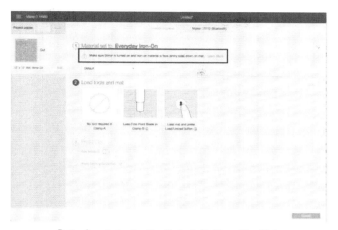

Design Space instruction tips. Photo via TheHomesIHaveMade

Again, if you click on Chipboard, Design Space will pop up instructions on the need to firmly secure your material, check the blade, or take some precautions.

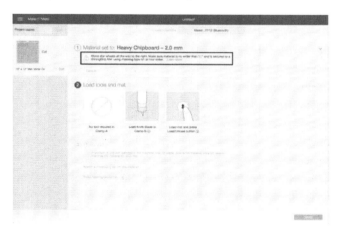

Design Space instruction tips. Photo via TheHomesIHaveMade

Don't ignore any of these instructions because you will mess up your design or waste lots of valuable time if you choose to ignore instructions.

Great work so far! One more step and you will be right here showcasing your first Cricut project. "Cricut Hacks" is what lies between you and your first project, and that's what you are going to learn in the next chapter.

6

CRICUT HACKS

There are lots of great designs to create through the Cricut Design Space if you really understand how the software truly works. In Chapter Two, you learned a few things about how you can master the Design Space Canvas Area. But to create wonderful Cricut designs, you need more than the regular panels and options within the Canvas. You need to get used to proven tips and tricks of creative designs, and that's what brought you here.

Stay attentive and remain focused as I take you through these wonderful Cricut Hacks.

1. Use Tin Foil to Sharpen Your Blade: Would you like to sharpen your blade and boost its life cycle at the same time?

Tin foil. Photo via Linds

You can achieve this if you sharpen your fine-point blade with tin foil. If you do, you'll make the blade perfect for any project you want to create and extend its life cycle by three times. How?

CRICUT HACKS | 201

Fine point blade. Photo via Linds

Take the blade out of its clamp and make its tip edge go through the tin foil 10 or 12 times.

Sharpening the blade via the Tin foil. Photo via Linds

2. Pick up Excess Vinyl with a Lint Roller: Crafters often waste time trying to clean up excess vinyl from their designs.

Picking excess vinyl from a design. Photo via Kayla

Some even end up messing up their project in the process. But this shouldn't pose any threat to you anymore because you can simply do it with a lint roller.

Putting excess vinyl on a lint roller. Photo via Kayla

With this roller, you can pick excess vinyl off your intricate designs with little or no effort at all. And, interestingly, as you weed excess small pieces on your design, you will save time. Also, you can use the roller to weed stray glitter off your workspace.

3. Easily Find a Fitting Font for Your Project: It's pretty easy to download fonts online. What is hard is finding the right font for your projects, and this requires skill and patience. But you don't have to face any difficulty while trying to find the perfect font for your project. Yes, with the "character maps" or "glyphs" on your PC, you can easily find a nice font for your Cricut project. How? Here's the how.

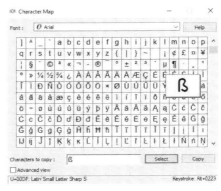

Selecting a font on a computer's character map

Go to the "Search" option on your PC > navigate "character map," if you are using Windows or "character viewer," if you are on Mac > click on your favorite font > scroll through to find the letter you like > select and copy the letter > open your Design Space Text box > paste the font there.

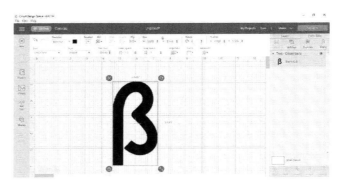

Inserting the font into Design Space

Here is another way to do this:

Go to wordmark.it > enter the word you want to search.

CRICUT HACKS | 203

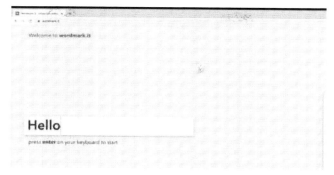

Finding a desired font via wordmark.it. Photo via Kayla

Go through the generated fonts > decide on the font to use.

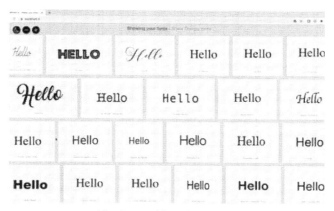

A list of generated fonts. Photo via Kayla

You can select some of the downloaded fonts but don't forget to save your selected options.

4. Simply Convert an Image to SVG: Sometimes, you find an image you love, but there is no way to use it for your Cricut designs. It hurts, but not anymore. Abbi (2018) knows how you can simply convert any image to SVG so that you can use the image in Cricut Design Space. How?

Uploading an image into Cricut Design Space. Photo via Kayla

Select the image you want to convert > save the image on your PC > navigate PNGtoSVG.com > upload the image via their "Choose File" option > reduce or increase the color count of the uploaded image, using the "+" or "-" button > click on the "Download SVG" button to have the already converted image on your PC > upload the image to your Design Space.

Selecting the image to upload. Photo via Kayla

5. Using a Weeding Box: What is a weeding box? It is just creating a box over an image in the Cricut Design Space.

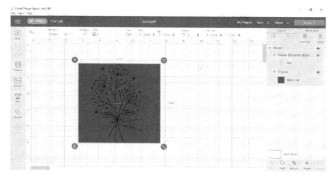

Creating a box over a design. Photo via Linds

So if you already have a box that will cut your Cricut image, what exactly should you do? Pick another shape > place it behind the box > click on the Attach button > cut the image at the point you want.

Ready-to-cut weeding box image. Photo via Linds

6. Add a Sewing Needle to a Mechanical Pencil to Weed Vinyl: You can weed excess vinyl in your Cricut design with a sewing needle and a mechanical pencil.

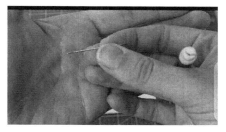

A sewing needle. Photo via Kayla

How? Grab a sewing Needle and a mechanical pencil > place the sewing needle inside the pencil > use it to weed the vinyl.

Make sure the pencil holds the needle firmly, or you'll have difficulties weeding the excess vinyl. Also, a weeding pen can do this task.

Using a mechanical pencil to weed excess vinyl. Photo via Kayla

7. Weed Excess Vinyl Using a Nail Polish Holder: You can weed excess vinyl with a nail polish holder.

A nail polish holder. Photo via Kayla

It works fine when you are weeding vinyl and you can also hang it in your craft room.

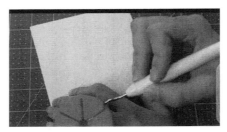

Using the polish holder to weed excess vinyl. Photo via Kayla

The nail polish holder is about $9 on Amazon.

A nail polish holder hung in a Cricut craft room. Photo via Kayla

8. Burnish and Remove Backing of Vinyl: Use a transfer tape to burnish and remove the backing of vinyl of your Cricut design.

Placing a transfer tape on a vinyl design. Photo via Kayla

It makes the process look so simple and amazing that you can run it right there in your home. So when you want to transfer your vinyl to the tape, place the design on a flat surface > spread the transfer tape on the vinyl > scrape the front of the tape two or three times > turn the design to scrape the back > carefully remove the transfer tape to pull out the vinyl.

Removing the transfer tape to pull out the vinyl design. Photo via Kayla

9. Add Mod Podge over Removable Vinyl: Do you want your removable vinyl to last longer? Add the vinyl to your blink and add mod podge on the surface of the design.

Mod podge. Photo via Kayla

With this, you can hold the vinyl firm on the design for a long time.

Applying the mod podge over the removable vinyl. Photo via Kayla

10. Use Stamp Designs on Scrap Vinyl: Using stamp designs on scrap vinyl is a fun Cricut hack that you can master in no distant time.

Stamp designs. Photo via Kayla

You can use a paper-cut stamp to do it. No, I don't know what other people call these stamps, but I saw lots of them on Amazon, and they come with different designs.

Selected stamp designs. Photo via Kayla

Feel free to make lovely Cricut projects with these stamp designs. How?

Paper designs being cut with the Stamps. Photo via Kayla

Place the stamp designs on your paper > punch it > cut different designs.

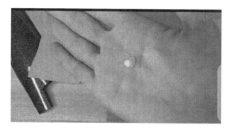

Cut-out paper designs. Photo via Kayla

11. Use a Dry Erase Marker to Line up Design: Do you know that you can center your vinyl design on a shirt? Yes, you can, and you only need dry erase markers and a couple of steps to create this design. Get the markers and follow these simple steps to line up your design.

Step 1. Fold the shirt in half and press the edges with a pressing iron.

Folded shirt. Photo via Kayla

Step 2. Grab the armpit over the shirt and fold it the other way round.

Folded shirt. Photo via Kayla

Step 3. Straighten the shirt on a flat surface.

Step 4. Fold the vinyl design in half but make sure you don't fold it on its sticky side.

Folded vinyl on a flat-lying shirt. Photo via Kayla

Step 5. Grab the dry erase marker and a ruler. Create a straight line on the design from its center.

Creating a straight line on a vinyl design. Photo via Kayla

Step 6. Line up the other direction, too, also from the center.

Step 7. Place the vinyl sheet on your shirt but make sure it is straight.

Placing vinyl design on the shirt. Photo via Kayla

Step 8. Erase the mark on the design and scrape it with a pressing iron for two or three minutes.

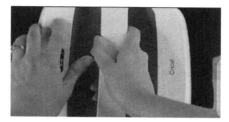

Using the Cricut EasyPress machine to press the shirt. Photo via Kayla

12. How to Change a One-layered Image into Two Layers: You will lose a lot of time if you want to work on multiple layers, one at a time. It is more difficult if you are crafting designs for commercial purposes. But there is a hack on how you can easily change one layer into two or more to aid speedy completion of your projects, and here's the hack. Change one layer into two or more layers, and you'll save yourself much stress. Fine. Even at that, this hack is simple and fun to do with a thumbnail. Select two layers—one with calligraphic color and the other with a solid color. Follow these simple steps to achieve this.

Step 1. Navigate Image in your Design Space > search for butterflies (or any image you like) > select the one you want to use > click on Enter.

Selecting butterfly images for a Cricut project. Photo via Kayla

You now have one layer image, but you can duplicate it or even use it to form as many layers as you want.

212 | BOOK 2

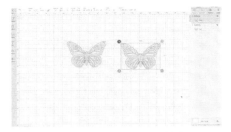

Duplicated butterflies. Photo via Kayla

Step 2. Duplicate the image > click on Contour > change the background of the first image to solid color > click on "X" at the top-right-hand corner to exit the image or simply click out.

Step 3. Change the color of the second image.

Changing the color of the images. Photo via Kayla

Step 4. Superimpose or drag the second image on the previous one.

The two images are superimposed to create one butterfly. Photo via Kayla

13. How to Weed "Brush" Style Fonts: Many complaints have been made about how difficult it is to weed or brush excess style fonts from a design. Some crafters mess up their projects, trying to make necessary adjustments.

A Cricut image. Photo via Kayla

But I have found a simple way to deal with those excess fonts without threatening the beauty of your designs. How? Use a lint roller to brush your style fonts to scrape off the little pieces.

Brushing the style font of the image. Photo via Kayla

Just make sure that your lint roller is not too sticky. You won't be able to pick the pieces if you are using a sticky lint roller. You can purchase your own lint roller via online market outlets like Amazon.

14. How to Get the Most out of Your Stickers on Print Then Cut: The size of your Print Then Cut on Cricut Design Space is often pegged at 9.25 by 6.75 cm. So, there is no way you can print anything larger than this measurement, even if you need to. But this shouldn't bother you at all because I have found a hack on how you can get the most out of your Print Then Cut. Just follow these simple steps.

Step 1. Open your Design Space and go to Shapes > select a Square > click on Unlock > set the maximum measurement size for the Print Then Cut. Use 6.75 by 9.25 cm for the measurement because that's the largest the Print Then Cut can make.

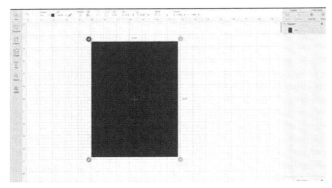

A Cricut shape. Photo via Kayla

Step 2. To design some stickers, launch Design Space on your PC > navigate Upload > find one or some of your SVG images on stickers > drag the selected image(s) into the Cricut Design Space. You may decide to increase the wideness of the selected image(s) if you want to. Consider making the image(s) two inches wide if that would add value to your design.

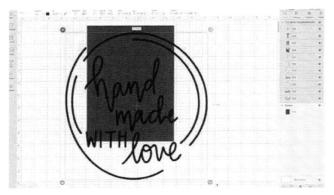

Placing the shape on a sticker. Photo via Kayla

Step 3. Go to Shapes > grab a Circle > place the selected image(s) in the Circle > change the color (if you need to) > highlight and center the Circle > upload or drag the design to the Cricut workspace.

CRICUT HACKS | 215

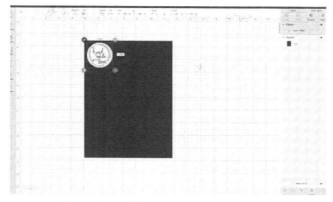

A Cricut sticker carefully placed in a rectangle. Photo via Kayla

Step 4. Reduce the design > duplicate the images until you get the number you want. Just make sure that the blade stays on whenever you are using the Print Then Cut option.

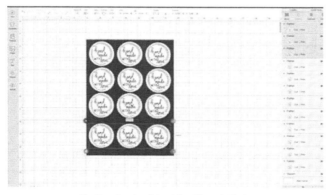

Duplicated copies of the sticker. Photo via Kayla

Step 5. Attach the stickers together and click on the "Make It" button.

216 | BOOK 2

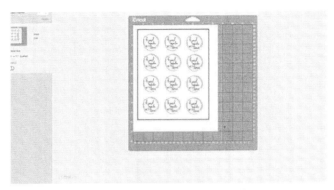

A group of attached stickers. Photo via Kayla

15. How to Save a Project as a PDF File: Cricut projects are normally stored within the Cricut Design Space, but I found a hack on how you can save your project as a PDF file. Let's pick it from the last hack I shared with you to make it easier and convenient.

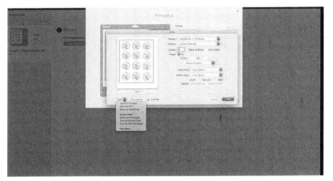

Saving the stickers as a PDF document. Photo via Kayla

From the Print Then Cut settings, click Continue > select Send to Printer > click on Use System Dialog > tap print to open a drop-down menu > tap PDF from the drop-down menu > select Save as PDF > create the name you want to use to save the document > click on Save.

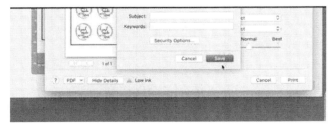

Drafting the subject and keywords of the PDF document. Photo via Kayla

The Cricut project will be saved as a PDF file in your document.

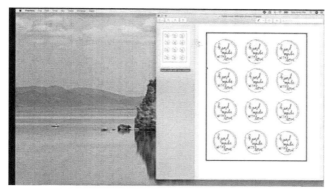

Stickers already saved in a PDF format. Photo via Kayla

16. Use Contact Paper to Make Glossy Stickers: Nothing stops you from using contact papers to create glossy stickers. Still, some crafters feel dejected when they are asked to create such designs. Since we are creating stickers again, we will be picking the process up from item "14." Remember, we made some duplicates last time, and we ended up with some stickers. But for this hack, you will have to delete all the stickers, except one. Good. So, get ready to make your own sticker glossy but not without these simple steps.

Step 1. Click on Make It > tap Continue > click on Change to Best Quality to make the sticker bold and radiant > send the image to the printer and print out a copy.

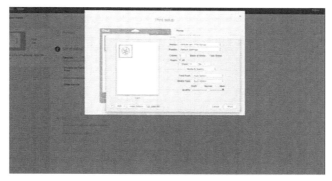

Sending and printing an image via a printer. Photo via Kayla

Step 2. Add a clear content paper over your mat sticker paper > do some test cuts to know which one works best > print out the clearest sticker > cut it out perfectly.

Placing a content paper on the printout design. Photo via Kayla

Step 3. Peel the content paper off the sheet > place it over your sticker but do it carefully so that you don't get too many air bubbles in it > scrape it down with your Cricut scraper to make sure there is no air bubble.

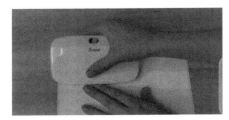

Scraping the content paper to prevent air bubbles. Photo via Kayla

Step 4. Load it into the Cricut machine so that the machine can cut it > pick up the sticker > keep the backing.

Running the glossy sticker via a Cricut machine. Photo via Kayla

I just love the glossy look on the sticker. Even if you get it wet, it won't smear at all.

17. Use Matte Tape to Cut Glossy Paper on Explore Air 2: Have you ever noticed that the Cricut Explore Air 2 always has difficulty cutting glossy paper? If you try it now, you will discover that the machine finds it difficult, if not impossible, to read the black registration lines on the stickers.

CRICUT HACKS | 219

Cutting a glossy paper via Explore Air 2. Photo via Kayla

The machine tends to come up with an error message, indicating that you have fed wrong details into the machine or the presence of a technical problem.

Error cut page for a glossy paper via Explore Air 2. Photo via Kayla

No worries. I will show you a trick on how to make this work.

Scotch magic tape. Photo via Kayla

Take Scotch tape > place it on the black registration lines > feed the glossy paper into the machine.

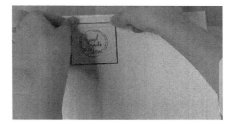

Placing the Scotch magic tape on the black registration lines. Photo via Kayla

220 | BOOK 2

The Cricut Explore Air 2 machine will recognize the paper and speed up the cutting process.

Finely cut glossy paper. Photo via Kayla

18. Use Remove.bg to Remove a Background: Crafters often complain about the tedious process of removing the background of images on Cricut Design Space. But I came across a hack on how you can easily do it via remove.bg with little or no effort, and I will be sharing the tip with you here.

Also, apart from the fact that the technique is easy and convenient, it's pretty cool and fun. Here is how to do it.

Step 1. Search Google for free butterflies or any images you want to use and click on one of the images.

Searching Google for free butterflies. Photo via Kayla

Step 2. Right-click the image and select Save out of the options that popped up.

Selecting and saving chosen butterfly image. Photo via Kayla

Step 3. Go to Upload on remove.bg and upload the image.

CRICUT HACKS | 221

Uploading the image on remove.bg. Photo via Kayla

Step 4. Double-click on the downloaded image and remove the background.

Removing the image background. Photo via Kayla

Step 5. Launch your Cricut Design Space> go to Upload > select the image with deleted background > click on Complex.

222 | BOOK 2

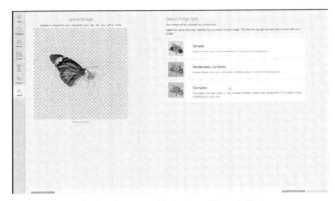

Uploading the image on Design Space. Photo via Kayla

Yes, you are clicking on Complex because the image you're working on is a complex one, not one you designed from scratch.

19. Have Multiple Cricut Machines Running at the Same Time: Do you know that you can have two or more Cricut machines connected to your PC, with all running at the same time? It is a great way to enhance your capacity and save loads of time, especially if you are running a big design business or having lots of things to attend to, besides crafting a few Cricut projects. How does this work? Just follow these simple steps.

Step 1. Upload a random design > bring the image to Design Space > change it to a dry image > click on Ungroup to edit the image the way you want > click on Make It.

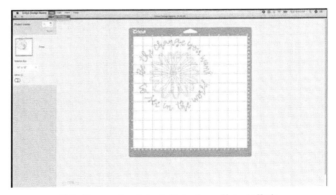

Uploading a random design to Design Space. Photo via Kayla

Step 2. Open a new window > use a different project or use the existing one > select the second machine > click on Make It.

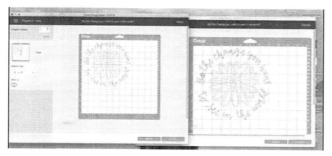

Selecting different Cricut machines on two Canvas' windows. Photo via Kayla

Step 3. Click On Continue on both screens.

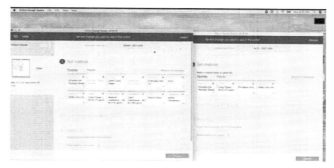

Setting up the Cricut machines. Photo via Kayla

You can use a USB to connect the machines to your PC or simply do a Bluetooth connection. Both machines can print at the same time.

20. Layer Vinyl Using Parchment Paper: Crafters usually find it hard to layer their vinyl designs, but there's a simple way to do it. You will need parchment paper to explore this hack. Follow these steps to use the paper to layer your vinyl.

Step 1. Put one of your layer pieces on the parchment paper.

Placing a layer piece on the parchment paper. Photo via Kayla

Step 2. Grab another piece of parchment paper > take your transfer tape > place the tape on one of the pieces you're going to be laying.

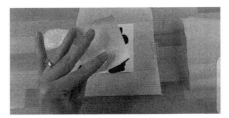

Scraping the side of the parchment paper. Photo via Kayla

Step 3. Grab the second parchment paper > place it on top of the black bottom layer of the vinyl.

Placing the second parchment paper on the bottom layer of the vinyl. Photo via Kayla

Do not cover all the pieces of the layer with parchment paper.

Step 4. Place each piece on the side that does not have the parchment paper. Just make sure it is lying perfectly.

Placing the pieces of the parchment paper side by side. Photo via Kayla

Step 5. Scrape the side until it looks fine, free of air bubbles > remove the parchment paper > take off the transfer tape.

CRICUT HACKS | 225

Scraping the side of the parchment paper. Photo via Kayla

Which hack is your favorite?

CONCLUSION

"Cricut Design Space for 2021 and Beyond: The Beginner's Step-by-Step Guide to Mastering Cricut Design Space in Just 21 Days" offered a careful but purposeful insight into Design Space: how to launch the software and create an account on it, how to use its tools and functions proficiently, especially in creating awesome DIY projects, how to take one's skills to greater heights, using Cricut hacks, and lots more. The six-chapter book had the right tips and tricks necessary to up your confidence and to make you a pro crafter in no time. How soon you turn to a pro crafter depends solely on how fast you learn and use the tricks and tips in this book.

Chapter One explored Design Space and how you could launch it on your Mac or Windows PC and iOS or Android device. There, you learned how to download, install, and launch the software on your favorite device, as well as how to get it uninstalled.

You also learned how to unwrap and set up a newly purchased Cricut machine: be it Cricut Maker, Cricut Explore, or Cricut Joy, subscribe for Cricut Access, and opt for the right Access plan.

Chapter Two left no stone unturned in a bid to help you master the Design Space Canvas Area. There, you saw lots of buttons and how to use them when designing a Cricut project. You learned a few shortcuts on how to create your unique projects effortlessly and in no time too!

Chapter Three took you through Projects in Design Space. You learned how to run specific functions while you are designing or creating a Cricut project.

You learned how to save, open, or edit Design Space projects on Desktop, how to save, open, or edit Design Space projects on the app, how to share Design Space projects on Desktop, iOS, or Android device; how to use Design Space templates, how to use Ready-to-Make Design Space projects, and how to design your own unique Ready-to-Make Design Space project.

Chapter Four focused on using images in Design Space. You learned that you could actually add images to your Cricut designs via your PC, iOS, or Android device. Remember you could

228 | CONCLUSION

click on "All Images," "Categories," or "Cartridges" to open a pool of amazing images and select the one(s) to use in your design.

Other significant things you learned in the chapter included how to browse and search for cartridges, how to search for cartridges with a filter, how to download Cricut cartridge online, how to purchase Cricut images via Mac or Windows PC and iOS or Android device, how to upload Basic or Vector images via PC and mobile device, how to edit images in Upload mode, and how to create Cricut layers and separate objects.

Chapter Five presented useful tips in Advanced Design Space that could help you master the software and create fascinating Cricut projects. Some of these tips are: Do some search terms' experiment; Check for more images from a chosen cartridge; Use free text and images; Change lines to Draw, Score, or Cut; Draw items about the mat; Save the Cut materials you always use; Connect several Cricut machines at once; Edit Cut settings for all your materials; Pay keen attention to instructions.

Does the last one sound funny? Yes, you can't master Design Space or create unique Cricut designs if you don't follow instructions. Remember I told you from the beginning that the ball was in your court. It is still there!

Chapter Six delved into Cricut hacks. Those pretty little hacks seemed hard to do but not for you anymore. Highlights of the chapter included how to add a layer to an image, how to use stamp designs on scrap vinyl, and how to save a Cricut project as a PDF file, and how to find a fitting file for your project.

You have all the tools to create a wonderful Cricut project. Take a bold step now and use the tools. Go create a project you can call our own!

We cherish and appreciate your support. Kindly leave a review on Amazon if you enjoyed reading this book.

REFERENCES

Causey, J. (2018, February 13). How to Use Slice and Weld in Design Space.

https://www.google.com/url?sa=t&source=web&rct=j&url=https://inspiration.cricut.com/how-to-use-slice-and-weld-in-design-space/&ved=2ahUKEwievLb005PvAhViaRUIHdi-QBewQtwIwD3oECC8QAg&usg=AOvVaw2S1-zXkOQrDWlFOm1timVo

Cricut Guide (N.D). How do I share my Design Space project?

https://help.cricut.com/hc/en-us/articles/360009377574-How-do-I-share-my-Design-Space-project-#:~:text=Enter%20your%20Cricut%20ID%20and,the%20bottom%20of%20the%20tile.

Cricut Guide (N.D). Uploading Images into Design Space.

https://help.cricut.com/hc/en-us/articles/360009556313-Uploading-Images-into-Design-Space#ios

Creative Crafts with Linds (2018, July 17). How to sharpen your cricut blade with tinfoil.

https://m.youtube.com/watch?v=Tw66SSFBF7Q

Kayla's Cricut Creations (2020, July 9). 20 Cricut Hacks I Learned on TikTok.

https://www.youtube.com/watch?v=-d8GiT3Ks_s&ab_channel=Kayla%27sCricutCreations

Mostella, H. (2017, December 26). Uploading an image into Design Space with iPhone/iPad.

https://m.youtube.com/watch?v=3eZZ3dArB7A

Nunemaker, L. (2017, November 18). How to upload images in Cricut Design Space from iOS App.

https://m.youtube.com/watch?v=2Lc8vjO6hB8

TheHomesIHaveMade (2019, April 23). 20 Cricut Design Space Tips & Tricks You'll Really Want to Know.

https://thehomesihavemade.com/2019/04/20-cricut-design-space-tips-tricks-youll-really-want-to-know/

BOOK 3

CRICUT PROJECT AND PROFIT IDEAS FOR 2021 AND BEYOND: THE BEGINNER'S STEP-BY-STEP GUIDE TO TONS OF PROJECT IDEAS AND MAKING MONEY FAST WITH CRICUT

© Copyright 2019 - All rights reserved.

It is not legal to reproduce, duplicate, or transmit any part of this document in either electronic means or in printed format. Recording of this publication is strictly prohibited and any storage of this document is not allowed unless with written permission from the publisher except for the use of brief quotations in a book review.

CLAIM YOUR BONUS

The Cricut Tool Kit
This is what you'll get in this Free tool kit:

1. Over 100 beautiful **SVG Files** that will spark your creativity

2. The Cricut Supplies Cheatsheet, with the most essential supplies you'll need for your first project

3. Access to our private Facebook group where you get to meet like-minded Cricut lovers and get tons of project ideas and tons of **free SVGs**

To claim your tool kit simply Click Here. Or Copy and paste this link into your browser: https://productiveplans.activehosted.com/f/7

INTRODUCTION

My friend, Olivia, saw me craft a giant papercraft for a friend, and she loved the artwork. Four days later, she called to say she'd love to see me craft a customized Iron-On t-shirt during her school's Art Club annual event billed for the next two days. "This year's event would be used to market the image of our school, and most of our parents would be attending," she informed me. *Perfect! I will also get a chance to show people how creative I am with Cricut projects*, I told myself.

An elated Olivia and her students watched me select a customized template for the project, shape, and size of my design, using the Cricut Design Space. Everyone kept cheering and applauding me from the moment I used my Cricut EasyPress 2 to press the Iron-On vinyl design on the t-shirt till the time I weeded excess vinyl from the surface of the design material. The whole design turned messy because I didn't allow it to cool down properly before I peeled off the carrier sheet. I heard someone say "what a mess" and the guests started heading straight to the exit door, one after the other. I knew Olivia would be mad at me. The incident motivated me to master all skills related to Cricut projects.

Maybe you're crafting a vinyl design on a mug. Fine, you've got all the supplies, including the ceramic mug, transfer tape, and scrapper. After you've cut the vinyl to shape, peeled the vinyl from the mat, scraped it, and completed all other steps, you're left with a totally messed-up vinyl-on-a-mug design. Soon, you realize it is another waste of effort, time, and money.

Perhaps your own project is a paper butterfly heart. You've downloaded your favorite paper butterfly heart template online, uploaded the template to your Design Space, and cut the butterfly designs. But you need each layer to stay separate because you're crafting a customized paper butterfly heart. The more you try to make the layers stay apart, the messier the layout looks like. For over an hour you try to fix it but you just can't and you never finished the anticipated project.

How badly did you need someone to tell you to watch out for the sticky side of the vinyl when you're about to spread it on your work surface? At least, if someone had said something, you wouldn't have messed up the design. Again, just imagine how great you'll feel when you've fully mastered Design Space and you know you could easily separate the layers of the paper butterfly heart by clicking the Ungroup button in your Design Space Canvas Area.

Once you've mastered the step-by-step guide for crafting Cricut projects you'll know you have to wait five minutes before you could touch the sticky side of your vinyl, let alone spread it on your work surface. By then, you'll be confident with your Design Space research skills and you'll know that you could simply tap the Ungroup button to separate the layers of your paper butterfly heart.

What do you stand to gain in this book?

- I will show you some fantastic Cricut project ideas and the materials you need to craft your favorite paper, vinyl, fabric, and infusible ink projects.
- I will show you a step-by-step guide for crafting Cricut projects such as a spider web garland, vinyl on mugs, cupcake wrappers with flowers, 3D candy cart, and lots more right at home.
- You will be exposed to the finest and most profitable Cricut crafts to sell and the best ways to market your Cricut projects to make tons of money from crafting.

Is there anything left to focus on? Yes, shift your focus to your confidence, concentration, and determination to use the tricks and tips of this book in real-life Cricut projects. Now is the time to breathe life into your ideas, create beautiful Cricut projects, sell them, and make lots of money.

How does that sound?

Your journey to crafting wonderful Cricut projects to sell takes us to gather lots pf project ideas with different materials in Chapter One.

I sincerely hope that you'll enjoy my book!

1

CRICUT PROJECT IDEAS AND THEIR MATERIALS

You need wonderful project ideas and inspiration to forge ahead to create your first project. Crafting can be fun when we share our project ideas with one another. This way, each and every one of us will be inspired to create something unique. Rather than relying only on your own ideas, you can create more appealing Cricut projects when other people share their project tricks with you.

How or where can you learn tricks? Right here, in this chapter, I will share with you five different and easy-to-understand Cricut craft ideas that you can practice from home. I will walk you through paper, heat transfer vinyl (HTV), vinyl, infusible ink, and fabric Cricut project ideas, and you will be able to master them all in no time. Use any Cricut machine for all the above project categories, but the Cricut Maker is more suitable for most fabric crafts. Just be creative. Don't allow your status as a newbie to stop you from using a different kind of fabric or paper.

PAPER CRAFTING IDEAS

Crafting, for most crafters, including newbies, starts with paper projects. Most of these crafters had to learn how to cut paper projects before they could turn to any other projects. Sure, paper projects often look simple, gorgeous, and beautiful, depending on the technique used. Check below for a few paper crafting ideas and the materials you will need to create them.

1. Cricut Paper Flowers: Here's a lovely project you can easily do to start. Yes, Cricut Maker is an ideal machine for the project, and you could use the Scoring Wheel to craft unique score lines on your Cricut paper flowers. Feel free to use a rainbow theme or simply customize the project your own way.

Cricut paper flowers. Photo via Kayla

Required Materials
Cricut Maker (Cricut Explore is also fine)
Scoring Tool or Scoring Wheel
Large cardstock
1.5" wooden half circles
4" and 6" Styrofoam rounds
Yellow spray paint
Hot glue
Yellow crepe paper

2. Printable Planner Stickers: Here's an amazing paper crafting project you can design on a daily basis.

Cricut planner stickers. Photo via Amazon

Crafting printable planner stickers is pretty cool and easy, but you're surely going to need a template for the stickers you want to create.

Cricut planner stickers. Photo via Amazon

Required Materials
Cricut Maker or Cricut Explore machine
Cricut sticker paper (printable vinyl too is okay)
Hole punch
1" binder

3. *Gingerbread Centerpiece*: True, this beautiful project is time-consuming, but it is perfect for every home, especially during holidays. Design a string of lights within the gingerbread if you want to make the project more appealing. Again, feel free to customize the project.

Cricut gingerbread Centerpiece. Photo via Michele Purin

Required Materials
String lights
11 (2mm) Cricut Kraft chipboard
Red cardstock
White 12 by 48 inches Cricut vinyl (2 rolls)
Gingerbread house project file (front and side)
Painter's tape (blue)
Transfer tape
6 sheets vellum
Cricut 12 by 12 mat

4. Pineapple Vase: Are you wondering about what you could send to your kids' teachers at the end of summer break? A pineapple vase makes for a sweet gift, and you can design it as a beginner's project.

Cricut pineapple vase. Photo via Amazon

    Required Materials
    Pineapple vase cut file (paper)
    Cute succulent
    Glue gun
    Cricut 12 by 14 cardstock
    Cricut single scoring wheel and cutting mat
    Cricut Maker and Fine Point Blade

5. Paper Pinwheels: Learn how to create paper pinwheels if you crave a creative way to décorate your home or make your parties stand out. Yes, pinwheels are perfect décorative designs and they are very easy to design. Depending on your choice, pinwheels could come in large or smaller sizes. Search for "pinwheel templates" online to download the one that suits your interest.

CRICUT PROJECT IDEAS AND THEIR MATERIALS | 241

Cricut paper pinwheels. Photo via Amazon

Required Materials
Scrapbook paper
Pencils
Hot glue
Glue gun
Small beads (buttons are fine too)
Cricut Maker (Cricut Explore can also be used)

6. 3D Paper Stars: Suitable for a craft room DIY wall art, 3D paper stars are eye-catching and beautiful. You will definitely enjoy creating this bundle of colorful designs on your own. Who says you can't start off with a beautiful project?

Cricut 3D paper stars. Photo via Amazon

Required Materials
Design Space star file
Cricut Maker
Deluxe paper foil (embossed)
Scoring wheel

7. Acorn Treat Box: Here is a cool gift for that person who's close to your heart. This project is not only easy, but also fun. With scrapbook papers and a few materials, you can design your own Acorn treat box. I will show you a list of paper materials you could use to create your Acorn treat box. Still, if it is hard to find these in your local craft store, just settle for any colored or fall-themed paper. Just make sure you love the color you're using.

Cricut Acorn treat box. Photo via Amazon

Required Materials
Brazzil cardstock, Orange Chevron, or Tan Chevron.
Paper glue
Ribbon
Cricut Maker or Cricut Explore

VINYL CRAFT PROJECT IDEAS

Once you've done some paper projects, use your Cricut machine to create adorable vinyl projects with little or no effort. The process of running vinyl craft projects via Cricut machine is fast and can be fun. It doesn't matter if you are not a designer yet. You still can create tons of lovely vinyl craft projects with Cricut Access.

What exactly is Cricut Access? Cricut Access holds all the fonts, images, and ready-to-make projects you need to create your projects. To learn how to subscribe and use Cricut Access, check my second book, *Cricut Design Space for 2021 and Beyond: The Beginner's Step-by-Step Guide to Mastering Cricut Design Space in Just 21 Days*.

Still, you can visit shop.cricut.com to get additional information on Cricut Access or choose a subscription plan. We will now consider a few craft project ideas and the materials you will need to create them.

1. Floral Vinyl Wall Art: The floral vinyl wall art is an eye-catching project you can create with your Cricut machine. It can give your walls and living spaces an amazing look, and you can create the design easily at this stage.

CRICUT PROJECT IDEAS AND THEIR MATERIALS | 243

Floral vinyl wall art design. Photo via Amazon

Required Materials
Cricut Air (other SVG compatible cutting machines can be used)
Floral SVG files
Removable indoor vinyl (black, 10 yards)
Weeder
Transfer tape
Scraper (extra large)
12" by 24" mat

2. DIY Acrylic Keychain: The DIY acrylic keychain is one project you should definitely try. The design comes with adhesive vinyl that is trendy. Again, you can easily personalize the design and present it as a gift to a loved one. This artwork is as easy to make as it is beautiful.

DIY acrylic keychain

Required Materials
Cricut machine
Weeding tool
Acrylic SVG file
Transfer tape
Needle nose plier
décorative tassel

3. Wood Lettering Board: Craft a wood design with your favorite vinyl lettering, and you will see why this project remains the choice of most crafters. Quote boards on walls and other parts of the house look great, but you need to use your creativity to spice up the design. Just make sure the words you select add value to the design.

Wood lettering design

Required Materials
Scraper tool
Weeding tool
Cricut vinyl
Transfer tape
Cricut permanent vinyl
Cricut machine
Sponge brush
Painter's tape
Paper plate
Wood sign
Acrylic paint

4. Pumpkin Doormat: A personalized Pumpkin doormat is a fantastic vinyl project you can do with your Cricut Explore Air 2 machine. It looks pretty cool, and it is a project that you don't need tons of guides to create. However, if you want to design your own pumpkin doormat, you will need patience. First-timers and newbies can find crafting aid on this project online.

A Cricut pumpkin Doormat

Required Materials
Cricut Explore Air 2
12" by 24" cutting mat
Cricut vinyl (stencil vinyl may be used too)
Contact paper
Polyurethane spray
Acrylic paint (black)
Masking tape

5. *Rustic Wall Sign*: If you have them, don't let those scraps of wood litter your back yard or garage. Instead, use them to create a DIY rustic wooden sign. Trust me; you will love this home décor because it is easy to design and personalize. Using creative painting and graphic work on these scraps creates enticing décor for your home.

A rustic wall sign

Required Materials
Painter's tape
Wood paint
Wood board
Vinyl
Cricut machine

6. Personalized Balloons: Here's a beautiful craft idea for all events and parties, especially those involving kids. Personalized balloons made from vinyl look really good and they are perfect gifts for kids. They are also fun and easy to design.

Personalized balloons

Required Materials
Cricut machine
Scraper
Transfer tape
Balloons
Vinyl
Weeder tool

A personalized Cricut ballons

7. Planner Stickers: Printable planner stickers can be made of vinyl and making one is fun. There are lots of sticker images available on Cricut Access. If you have not subscribed to a Cricut Access plan and you still want to create a planner sticker, you can start from scratch. There is nothing wrong with that, since you know how to create it. There are tons of online aids to guide you through the process of crafting your own planner stickers. If you need help on how to craft the design, search for "how to craft a planner sticker" in your search engine of choice.

CRICUT PROJECT IDEAS AND THEIR MATERIALS | 247

Required Materials
Cricut machine
Matte
Cricut sticker paper
Light grip mat
Printer
Weeding tool

8. Customized Backpack: Are you wondering about what you could create as a back-to-school design for your kid? A customized backpack is a great idea, which can tell kids to be kind to one another.

Required Materials
Transfer tape
Weeder tool
Backpack
Cricut premium vinyl
Cricut Maker

9. DIY Wooden Frame Clock: A DIY wooden frame clock is a beautiful vinyl project you will love to make. Yes, apart from being a great home décor, the wooden frame clock is a charming gift for family and friends. You will love crafting your own DIY wooden frame clock because it's pretty easy to create.

Required Materials
Cricut machine
Vinyl
Clock assembly kit
Wooden frame
Craft knife
Plaid chalk paint
Scrapbook paper
Paintbrush

10. Candy Cart: Here's is a fun and beautiful Cricut paper project you can design anywhere, anytime. It is actually a 3D project you can design for special occasions, such as the perfect Valentine's gift for your spouse.

Candy cart. Photo via Mandee

Required Materials
Cardstock
Cricut Maker or Cricut Explore machine
Candy cart SVG file or template

Dura-Lar film
décorative Gems
Hot Glue

HEAT TRANSFER PROJECT IDEAS

Heat transfer vinyl, also known as Iron-On vinyl, makes crafting easy and versatile. You can use Iron-On vinyl to create tons of fun projects and also spice up your designs with paper, canvas, fibers, wood, and fabrics. Again, you need just an iron or a Cricut EasyPress machine to stylishly and creatively apply your vinyl.

Below, you'll find some heat transfer projects that you can create whenever you feel like being creative.

1. Unicorn Birthday: Do you know that you can design a birthday shirt for a lady using the unicorn SVG file and a blank t-shirt? Rather than worrying about the right design to purchase, why don't you just create a beautiful unicorn birthday t-shirt for your daughter? You can customize the shirt to make it unique for her, but you will need to up your creativity a bit.

Required Materials
Blank t-shirt
Cricut Maker (Cricut Explore Air 2 is also fine)
Cricut EasyPress 2 machine
Weeding tools
Iron-On expressions vinyl

2. DIY Rain Boots: Every year has its rainy season. Feel free to design and customize adorable Iron-On DIY rain boots for yourself and your little ones. Crafting Iron-On vinyl on rubber boots is super easy.

Required Materials
Cricut EasyPress 2
Rubber rain boots
Hand towel
EasyPress tote
Iron-On vinyl

3. Leather Monogram Charms: Would you like to use your new hobby to create a Christmas stocking accessory or gift? Leather monogram charms come with a great look and you can personalize them to suit your needs. Also, you can easily create your own leather monogram charms to show off your skills.

Required Materials
Knife blade
Iron-On vinyl
Cricut genuine leather
Cricut Maker

4. Birth Stat Elephant: Here is a cute baby gift. You can customize the design, and creating one is lots of fun. You can create your own adorable birth stat elephant, or make one for one of your friends.

Required Materials
Iron-On vinyl
Cricut EasyPress mat and EasyPresss 2
Weeding tools
Cricut Maker
Elephant artwork

5. Grandma's Kitchen Towel: Is it too early to start preparing for Mother's day gifts? Not at all! Sure, the earlier you start, the better it's likely to work. A quick, easy, and fun project, like the Grandma's Kitchen Towel can save your time and energy.

Required Materials
Cricut Maker (Cricut Explore Air 2 can also be used)
Flower sack towel
Gray HTV
Cricut EasyPress and EasyPress mat
Sweet mint HTV
SVG file

6. *Iron-On Socks*: You can also use Iron-On to customize your socks. The project is so easy that you can finish it in under 20 minutes, depending on how colorful you want your socks to look.

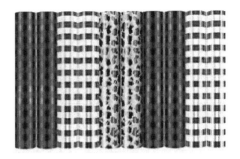

Required Materials
Cricut machine and Design Space
Pink foil Iron-On
Weeding tools
A pair of socks
Fine Point Blade
Cricut EasyPress 2
12" by 12" standard grip mat

7. *Custom Gloves*: DIY customized gloves come with Iron-On vinyl patterns which can be made to look vibrant. These gloves can be made to look either simple or fancy, and you'll fall in love with them.

Required Materials
Cricut Maker
Cricut EasyPress 2
Patterned Iron-On vinyl
Fabric gloves

CRICUT PROJECT IDEAS AND THEIR MATERIALS | 253

FABRIC CRAFT IDEAS

At this stage, it is easy to create fabric craft projects, since Cricut machines hardly encounter challenges when cutting fibers and fabrics. As usual, I will show you a few fabric craft projects you can design. Whether you intend to work on these at home or at a friend's place, you can create your own fancy fabric craft projects with little or no guidance at all. Still, I recommend Cricut Maker for most of these projects. Other machines may not give you the same quality you get with the Maker.

1. Key Ring: Tons of time will be saved when you create this simple project with your Cricut Maker. Again, the key ring has a beautiful look, and it is a good gift for someone close to your heart.

Required Materials
Pink fabric mat
Fabric
Key Ring hardware
Pattern
Webbing
Cricut Maker

2. Makeup Bag: Check out this gorgeous and lovely DIY makeup bag. It is an envelope purse look-alike, and Cricut newbies will create it with little to no effort at all. In less than 20 minutes, you're done with your own makeup bag. Wow!

Required Materials
Cricut Maker
Cricut rotary blade
12" by 24" fabric cutting mat
Cricut fabric
Cricut sewing kit
Cricut EasyPress 2
Washable fabric pen
Cricut brayer

3. Leather Hair Accessories: I love long hair and I think most women also admire having a lot of hair. A few years ago, a friend told me I could grow my hair using a herbal local hair-enhancing cream. She told me she'd used the herbal mixture for three years. And, seeing how long her hair had grown, I quickly purchased the cream and started using it. I saw significant results three weeks after I started using the hair enhancer. I have a lot of hair and lots of things to do to keep it looking good. I have to wash, condition, and brush my hair regularly.

Do you also face these extra responsibilities? I have great news for you! You can create lovely ribbons, bows, or hair ties to adorn your hair. You can show off your hair with leather accessories, so it stays beautiful all day long. Just a few materials stand between you and your own leather hair accessories.

Required Materials
Cricut Maker
Cricut knife blade
Chopstick
Hair clips
Headbands
Cricut felt
E6000 adhesive
Genuine or metallic leathers

4. Easy Felt Flowers: Some newbie crafters don't know that a Cricut machine can cut felt. Not only can you cut felt with your machine, but you can also create beautiful felt flowers with your Cricut Maker or Cricut Explore Air 2 machine.

Required Materials
Cricut Maker or Cricut Explore Air 2
Felt flower SVG file
Glue gun
Cricut felt sampler
Cricut cutting mat

5. Leather Journals: Here is a beautiful mini-leather journal you can create and present to a loved one. Apart from being an amazing gift no one can turn down, a leather journal is a work of art. Despite its intricate design, the journal is extremely easy to make.

Required Materials
Cricut Maker
Fine Point Blade
Scoring wheel
Cricut faux leather (opt for your favorite color)

Cricut Iron-On foil
Cricut EasyPress mat and EasyPress 2
Rubber cement glue
Cricut bright pad

6. Simple Coaster: How about a simple coaster design? It is a beautiful holiday décor that looks amazing on your table or bar. Simple coasters are really easy to make. Designing one with the Cricut Maker machine is super exciting. Make yourself or a friend a set of these fun coasters.

Required Materials
Pinking and sharp scissors
Cricut fabric mat
Rotary blade
Fabric pen
Iron
Wool felt
Cricut Maker
Cotton fabric

7. Baby Burp Cloth: A baby burp cloth is an amazing fabric craft project idea. You can use your Cricut Maker to create a nice design. First, you'll have to design and cut a well-shaped baby burp pattern using your Cricut Maker. Then, use the pattern to sew your favorite baby burp cloth.

CRICUT PROJECT IDEAS AND THEIR MATERIALS | 257

Required Materials
SVG pattern for a burp cloth
1/4 yard flannel fabric (2 pieces)
12" by 24" fabric grip mat
Rotary blade
Cricut Maker
Gutermann thread

8. Fabric Luggage Tags: Fabric luggage tags are a useful project if you travel a lot. They are also easy to make and can make a great gift for the traveler in your life.

Required Materials
Cricut Explore Air
12" x 12" fabric squares
Cricut Design Space
Iron-On vinyl
Ribbon
StrongGrip mat and StandardGrip mat
Iron

9. *Leather Earrings*: You can create beautiful DIY leather earrings with your Cricut or Silhouette machine. Leather earrings are so simple that you can make them even as a beginner. You can customize the design to make them in the style you or your best friend likes to wear.

Required Materials
Faux leather
Jewelry jump rings and ear wires
Cricut machine
Pliers

CRICUT INFUSIBLE INK PROJECT IDEAS

Infusible ink projects are unique but easy-to-make designs you can create at home. Just create the design, cut, and press it on your fabric. Make sure that the fabric-infused design won't wash off. Let's see two amazing Cricut infusible ink projects that you can easily create or design.

1. Mermaid Tote Bag: Here is a lovely DIY Mermaid infusible ink tote bag that you can design in just 30 minutes! You read right, it doesn't even take an hour to create this tote bag.

Required Materials
Cricut Maker or Cricut Explore Air 2
Cricut StandardGrip mat
Mermaid SVG files
Cricut 12" by 10" EasyPress 2
Cardstock
Big tote bag (blank)
Lint roller
Cricut infusible ink transfer sheet
Butcher paper (already has Infusible Ink rolls)
EasyPress mat

2. Infusible Ink Mouse Pad: Like the mermaid tote bag, this infusible ink mouse pad is another great beginner project you can create effortlessly. Research online for infusible ink tips and guides before you start creating your own infusible ink mouse pad, or you'll have a few ink issues to contend with.

Required Materials
Cricut EasyPress mat and EasyPress 2
Cricut Maker
White cardstock
Butcher paper
Cricut infusible ink transfer sheet
Mousepad

With these Cricut project ideas, I hope you are inspired to start creating your own wonderful projects. Are you wondering how to create these beautiful Cricut projects? When you get to Chapter Five, you will learn how to create tons of amazing projects.

BEST CRICUT CRAFTS TO SELL

It's fine if you own a Cricut machine and use it as a hobby. But you can craft amazing Cricut projects with your machine and make some cash. Everyone has their reasons for purchasing a Cricut machine. While some people purchase the machine to have a new hobby, others do it to start a business. There are people who initially start crafting as a hobby, but later venture into the business side of it. Some are making lots of money. You can use your Cricut machine and Cricut Design Space to design beautiful projects and earn money while doing what you love.

How do you know the best crafts to sell on the crafting market? I have about 100 well-researched Cricut Crafts you can design and sell for the most returns. But, for ease of reference, check the table below for the finest Cricut crafts to sell.

Cricut Project	Best Crafts to Sell
Paper crafts	Paper flower bouquets, corsages, cupcake toppers, standing paper flowers, party hats, party banners, favor boxes, princess centerpieces, die cuts, paper lanterns, gift tags, crepe paper flowers, paper bows, paper fans, geometric wall art, shadow boxes, paper flower crowns, embroidery hoop wreath, planner stickers, fairy houses, paper scenes, packaging stickers, and fairy houses.
Adhesive vinyl crafts	Custom mugs, hand lettered signs, tumblers, birth stats board, calendar or menu board, makeup brush holders, growth chart, monogram notebooks, custom balloons, monogram plates, license plates, dog bowls, vinyl clipboards, kitchen labels, stove cover, jewelry dishes, wood signs, door mats, custom cake stands, and dog treat jar.
Iron-On vinyl crafts	Tote bags, t-shirts, cutting boards, baby onesies, custom socks, drawstring bags, makeup bags, wood hangers, hot pads, tea towels, beer cozies, hats, aprons, bath towels, blankets, canvas shoes, and garden signs.
Woodcrafts	Cake topper, earrings, key chains, wood ornaments, family tree, coasters, and wood letters for signs.
Fabric crafts	Cosmetic bag, sleep masks, kids alphabet letters, drawstring bag, tassel garland, leather earrings, hair bows, leather journal cover, bunting banner, dolls, and soft toys, felt flowers, leather wallet, doll clothes, and burp cloths.

Sellable Cricut projects are not limited to the above. Feel free to study your local market to see what could add value to the consumers. You could sample consumers' opinions via social media and check craft forums.

Now that you know what crafts you can make and the best ideas to sell them, you made a great step towards crafting your own Cricut projects and starting a craft business. In the next chapter, I included a step-by-step guide for crafting many Cricut projects.

2

A STEP-BY-STEP GUIDE FOR CRICUT PROJECTS

Did you just purchase a Cricut machine and are wondering what to make with it and how? This is the right spot for you. Here, you get to easy-to-understand, step-by-step guidelines on how you can create lots of adorable Cricut projects. Grab a comfy seat, relax, and learn how to design these projects in sequence.

DIY GREETING CARD

Here is a gift card for anyone close to your heart. Most beginners are thrilled to create this lovely paper project because it looks cool, beautiful, and handy. Again, depending on your creativity level, you can improve the look of your design or even customize it. Use your imagination and creativity to embellish your own DIY Greeting Card with glitter and patterned cardstock décorations.

Again, since all standard cards are 5" by 7", you can mail your DIY greeting cards in regular envelopes.

Required Materials
Cricut Maker
Fine-Point blade
StandardGrip mat
Greeting Card SVG file
8.5" by 11" cardstock (65 lb.)

Instructions

Just follow these simple steps to create your own DIY Greeting Card.

Step 1. Download and unzip (if necessary) the greeting card SVG file online or get it from Cricut Access if you have a Cricut Access subscription plan.

Step 2. Upload the SVG file to Cricut Design Space. Go to Cricut Design Space on your computer > click on Upload > tap on Upload Image > select the downloaded SVG file > tap Save. Go to Recently uploaded images to tap the image, and click on Insert Images.

Step 3. Cut the greeting card design. Fix the fine-point blade to your Cricut machine and position a piece of cardstock, in a landscape pattern, on the StandardGrip mat.

Click on Make It > tap on Continue > select 'Cardstock' as material type and 'Default' as pressure option > cram the mat into your Cricut machine > click on Go to start cutting.

Just remember that you will use two sheets of cardstock for each card. Get ready to load the second sheet of cardstock, following the above process.

Step 4. Grab and remove your cardstock from the StandardGrip mat. Flip the mat, making its face lie on the work surface > carefully bend the mat up a bit from the material to remove it.

Step 5. Fold the card into two equal halves. Feel free to décorate it as you want.

You've just crafted your own DIY Greeting card!

DIY LABEL

A DIY label is one of the most effective projects for Cricut newbies. It is a perfect label for any event because you can customize the artwork. It is so simple that anyone can create it with little to no help at all. With a functional Cricut machine and a few other tools, you can design your own DIY label. Grab these supplies first.

Required Materials
Weeding tool
Cricut Joy
Transfer tape
Cricut Joy smart vinyl
A pair of scissors
A container to press the label on

Instructions

Just follow these simple steps to craft your own DIY label.

Step 1. Launch Design Space on your computer or mobile device > open a blank document > navigate the left sidebar to locate the text tool > open the text entry box by clicking on the text tool.

Step 2. Add your favorite text for the DIY label. Feel free to change the font if you don't like the current one. Also, you can resize the label, change its font size, or simply drag the text box from its four corners until you get your favorite shape and look. My personal favorite font is Cricut Sans. It looks clean and it is very easy to read. If you have different tastes, pick another font.

Step 3. Click on Make It. Place your vinyl below the guides on either side of your trail to load it into your Cricut Joy. You don't need a mat to run this task. The screen will show prompts that tell you that the vinyl was inserted and your machine continues from there.

Step 4. Click on the Go button. The button gets activated as soon as you load the vinyl.

Step 5. Hold the roll of vinyl > cut the new label with your scissors > weed excess vinyl from the four corners of the label > pull the label back to show the word(s) you want to print.

Step 6. Grab the transfer tape > cut it > carefully remove the backing of the transfer tape > place it on the label > gently run your palms on it to adhere the letters to the tape > pull up the tape > press the label on your favorite container > carefully remove the white backing of the tape.

You just designed a labeled container! Reading all the above probably made you think the process lasts forever. In reality, you need only five minutes to launch the software and complete the project.

VINYL ON MUGS

A crafter who doesn't know how to apply vinyl designs on mugs can't call themselves a crafter. Vinyl on mugs projects are colorful, customizable designs and make great gifts. Right from the comfort of your home, you can make your favorite vinyl designs on mugs. Let's see what we need and how to do it.

Required Materials
Ceramic mugs (don't opt for textured or powder-coated mugs)
Cricut cutting mat
Transfer tape
Scrapper
Rubbing alcohol
Fine-Point blade
Oracal 651 (or any other outdoor adhesive vinyl)
Vinyl on mug SVG files
Cricut machine

Instructions

Follow these simple steps to craft your own vinyl on mugs projects.

Step 1. Download vinyl on mug SVG files online or via Cricut Access. Select the file you want to use and upload it to Design Space, using the **Step 2** instruction on how to create a DIY Greeting Card.

Step 2. Cut the vinyl to shape. Spread the adhesive vinyl on your cutting mat, shining color side facing up, and use your fine-point blade to cut it. As soon as you finish cutting the vinyl, flip the vinyl on your cutting mat, and carefully peel the vinyl from the mat.

Step 3. Use the scraper to remove excess vinyl and transfer the design to your mug using the transfer tape. Cut the transfer tape into the size of the design > remove the backing of the transfer tape > stick the tape on the front side of your vinyl decal > transfer the vinyl to the mug. Watch out for the sticky side of the vinyl. If you mistakenly place it on your work surface, it will bend out of shape.

Step 4. Apply the vinyl. Use rubbing alcohol to clean the surface of your mug > create small edge snips round your transfer tape to blend the vinyl decal with the mug > apply your vinyl from the edges of the mug.

Step 5. Remove the transfer tape. You're good to go!

For the beautiful designs you get, this is surely an easy and convenient process that even complete beginners can do.

IRON-ON T-SHIRT

You may want to design an Iron-On t-shirt with your Cricut machine. This is yet another project that is extremely easy to do. Here are the materials you need to create your own, whether simple or fancy Iron-On t-shirt.

Required Materials
Iron-On vinyl
Weeding tool
StandardGrip mat
A cotton T-shirt
Cricut kraft knife
Cricut EasyPress 2
Cricut Maker

Instructions

Just follow these simple steps to create your own Iron-On t-shirt:

Step 1. Get a t-shirt design or create your own design. To get a ready-to-make design, launch Design Space > tap New Project > click on Templates > select Classic T-Shirt > choose your favorite style, size, and color. Use the template to shape and size your design, and click on Make It.

Step 2. Use the Iron-On vinyl to cut your t-shirt design. Place the design on your cutting mat, press the shiny side of your Iron-On vinyl on it, and do the cutting.

Step 3. Eliminate the excess vinyl from your t-shirt design.

Step 4. Press the design to your T-shirt using your Cricut EasyPress 2 machine. Just position the design on your t-shirt and press the design with your Cricut EasyPress 2 machine. Allow the design to cool down before you Peel off the carrier sheet. Still, for more information and application guidelines for your material, don't hesitate to visit Cricut at www.cricut.com.

You just designed your own Iron-On t-shirt. If you'd like to wash it before wearing, you can do that 24 hours after you finish applying the vinyl. Again, to avoid color bleeding, make sure you turn the shirt inside out before putting it in the washer.

IRON-ON ADOPTION BANNER

Iron-On vinyl, also known as heat transfer vinyl (HTV), isn't just for fabrics, as many Cricut newbies may erroneously believe. Just as you can use Iron-On vinyl to design a cute t-shirt, it can be combined with cardstock to create a banner, just like this beautiful adoption banner. Would you like to create and sell a unique banner for weddings, engagements, and other joyous occasions? This Iron-On adoption banner is the perfect design!

Required Materials
Ribbon
Cricut Maker or Cricut Explore
Cricut EasyPress 2
White cardstock
Gold glitter Iron-On vinyl

Instructions

Just follow these simple steps to create your own Iron-On Adoption Banner.

Step 1. Use your Cricut Maker or Explore machine to cut the cardstock into 5" by 7". Feel free to adjust the size as you want.

Step 2. Cut your glitter Iron-On vinyl and eliminate excess space.

Step 3. Arrange the Iron-On vinyl pieces on the already cut-to-size cardstock.

Step 4. Use the Cricut EasyPress 2 machine to stick the Iron-On vinyl to the cardstock flag.

Step 5. Carefully remove the plastic coating and plastic liner of the Iron-On material.

Step 6. Use the ribbon to string loose ends together.

I hope you ended up with a product you love!

PAPER BUTTERFLY HEART

A paper butterfly heart is lovely wall art that you can create at home. It also works as a gift to a friend or family member. Crafting your own paper butterfly heart shouldn't pose any challenge once I show you how to make it.

Required Materials
SVG file for paper butterfly heart
Tacky glue
Cricut mat
Fine-Point blade
8.5" by 11" cardstock (four sheets)
12" by 12" cardstock (any color)
16" by 20" stretched canvas
Pencil
Ruler
Cricut Maker or Cricut Explore Air 2

Instructions

Just follow these simple steps to create your own paper butterfly heart.

Step 1. Download the SVG file for paper butterfly heart online or via Cricut Access and upload the file to your Design Space.

Step 2. Arrange and cut your butterfly designs. Click on "Make It" if you want to cut your butterfly. Should you want to customize each layer separately, click on Ungroup. Just remember that you are using two mats (one for the 12" by 12" cardstock and the other one 8.5" by 11" cardstock). Repeat the cut until you get the desired number of butterflies. Use the fine-point blade to cut the materials.

Step 3. Remove the butterflies from the mat and pinch with your fingers to fold them.

Step 4. Use your pencil to trace a heart on the canvas. Measure the height and width of your canvas with a ruler to locate the middle point of your canvas. Draw the heart shape from the middle point.

Step 5. Glue your paper butterfly heart design. Randomize the position of the butterflies to create an overlapping effect > pay close attention to pencil lines > position the butterflies > apply the glue from the bottom.

Step 6. Clean up every visible line on the design.

Congratulations! You just completed creating your own paper butterfly heart.

INFUSIBLE INK LAYERED T-SHIRT

Infusible Ink layered t-shirts do not flake, peel, or crack, and they also look great on people. Crafting these shirts is very easy and you can personalize or customize them just the way you like them. They can make great presents, as well. Let's go and design your own colorful Infusible Ink layered t-shirt.

Required Materials
SVG file for infusible ink layered t-shirt
Butcher paper
StandardGrip mat
Cricut EasyPress machine
Infusible Ink t-shirt
Cardstock
Scissors and tweezers
Cricut Maker or Explore Air 2
Infusible Ink transfer sheets (use your favorite colors)

Instructions

Just follow these simple steps to create your own infusible ink layered t-shirt.

Step 1. Download your SVG file or create one yourself. To get a template for the project, launch Design Space on your computer > tap New Project > click on Templates > opt for 'Classic T-Shirt' > select your favorite color, size, and style > click on Make It, and print the design on your cardstock.

Step 2. Place the infusible ink transfer sheets on the cutting mat, blur side facing up. Spread your design on it and cut.

Step 3. Weed negative areas off your infusible ink design.

Step 4. Spread the infusible ink t-shirt on a flat surface > apply the infusible ink > use the Cricut EasyPress machine to stick the design to the project.

Step 5. Peel off the backing of the design as soon as it cools down a bit.

I'm sure that you'll love your new t-shirt! Customized t-shirts are really beautiful.

Woven Basket

Check out this woven basket and you'll agree that it is truly intricate and beautiful. Woven baskets are a fun project you can create on your own. Just ready the supplies and you're good to go.

Photo via Mandee

Required Materials
Cricut Maker or Explore machine
Cardstock
Woven Basket SVG template
Glue stick
Hot glue

Instructions

Just follow these simple steps to create your own woven Basket.

Step 1. Find and download the SVG template online.

Step 2. Launch your Cricut Design Space > upload the template > print out the template.

Step 3. Place the template on your cardstock > cut out the pieces of the basket.

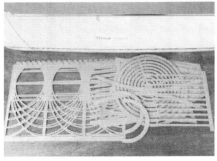

Photo via Mandee

A STEP-BY-STEP GUIDE FOR CRICUT PROJECTS | 271

Step 4. Place the two side pieces side by side > attach the pieces with your glue stick, one over the other > weave and alternate the strips of the bottom piece over the other piece.

Step 5. Grab the sides of the basket and fold everything up > glue the already folded up sides to the first pieces to form rounded corners > attach the basket handle.

Photo via Mandee

Step 6. Curve the edges of the basket to design a column and glue all the edges.

That's it! Now you have a beautiful woven basket to show off!

DIY GIANT PAPER FLOWER

Paper flowers can be dainty, but a DIY giant paper flower takes this to the next level. Most people encounter this wonderful craft design during events such as weddings, baby showers, and other special occasions. Feel free to create or customize your own DIY giant paper flower because it is both fun and simple to design.

Required Materials
Cricut Maker or Explore machine
SVG file template for DIY giant paper flowers
Glue gun
Wood dowel
Scissors
65 lb cardstock
Pencil

Instructions

Just follow these simple steps to create your own DIY Giant Paper Flower.

Step 1. Download your SVG template online > upload it to your Design Space > click on Make It > print out the template > lay it on the cardstock > trace the petals using your pencil. However, you need to determine the size and layer of each petal before you cut the cardstock. Take a look at the table below to figure it out.

Petal Size	Cut	Petal Measurement (inches)
Large (1st layer)	6 to 8	5.5 by 7.7
Medium (2nd layer)	6 to 7	3.9 by 5.3
Small (3rd layer)	6	3.0 by 4.1
Extra small (4th layer)	5 to 6	2.5 by 3.7
Extra large	6 to 8	7.5 by 10.5

Step 2. Stack 2 or 3 sheets of cardstock > cut the petals once you finish tracing them > create 1 1/2 inches slit at the rear end of each petal.

Step 3. Overlap the slit, starting with your first layer > add glue to the inside edge of each slit and the petals > curl the back of the petals, using the wood dowel.

Step 4. Grab a petal and add glue to its outer edge > overlap another petal, 45° to the previous petal > add another petal till you reach the last one, following that sequence.

Step 5. Alternate the 2nd, 3rd, and 4th layer of petals, one after the other to design the Giant Paper Flowers' Pompom Center.

Step 6. Use your scissors to cut the paper down, from the middle > keep the pieces apart > glue the edge of the first piece and roll it > add the next piece.

Step 7. Glue the center of the flower.

This is it! You have just designed your own DIY giant paper flower. I hope you love it!

DIY VALENTINE'S DAY WREATH

This is a nice project to make before Valentine's Day. This wreath is a fun and lovely craft you hang at home for your Valentine. The heart-shaped design can serve as cool home décor as well. Your imagination is the limit when customizing this project.

Required Materials
Cricut machine
Glue
Ribbons (fabric, twine, or yarn could be used)
Beautiful heart SVG file
Wreath

Instructions

Just follow these simple steps to create your own DIY Valentine's Wreath.

Step 1. Use a variety of ribbon, yarn, or twine to swaddle the wreath.

Step 2. Download the heart SVG file online or through Cricut Access.

Step 3. Launch Design Space on your computer > upload the SVG file > set the layout as you want and create the design for your project > print the design via your Cricut machine. Just vary the colors and sizes of the hearts to make the design fit the Valentine's Day theme.

Step 4. Lay the hearts on the wreath (as desired) > glue the hearts > add additional ribbons to spice up the design > customize it with a lovely Valentine's Day gift tag.

This way, you have a nice wall art for Valentine's Day in no time!

CUPCAKE WRAPPERS WITH FLOWERS

Cupcake wrappers are as fun as they look cute. What's even better is that there are lots of wrapper templates available for free on Design Space. Make sure you pick your favorite paper colors as you customize your own cupcake wrappers.

Required Materials
Cricut Explore
Tape
12" by 12" StandardGrip mat
Cardstock (multiple colors)

Instructions

Just follow these simple steps to design your own cupcake Wrappers with Flowers.

Step 1. Use the cupcake wrapper template to make a test cut to see if the sizing is perfect for you.

Step 2. Spread the cardstock on your StandardGrip mat > load the mat into your Cricut machine > pay attention to on-screen instructions to properly cut the cupcake wrappers.

Step 3. Muffle the cupcake wrapper and tape the edges.

Step 4. Use your desired flower designs on the wrapper.

Just like that, you have crafted your own cupcake wrappers with flowers.

SPIDERWEB GARLAND

Here's a paper-cut spider-web design you can easily create at home. Most crafters design it for Halloween, but feel free to customize it to use on t-shirts, vinyl, and other crafts. Let's find out how to make a garland below.

Required Materials
Cricut machine
SVG sample for Spiderweb Garland
12" by 12" StandardGrip mat
Black cardstock
Glue

Instructions

Just follow these simple steps to create your own Spiderweb Garland.

Step 1. Download the SVG sample online or through Cricut Access.

Step 2. Launch Design Space on your computer and upload the SVG sample.

Step 3. Position the cardstock on the StandardGrip mat > load the mat into your Cricut machine > pay attention to the on-screen guidelines and cut the design.

Step 4. Apply glue to the spiderweb pieces > keep the design in a safe place to dry up. Still, if the dried glue shows on the finished piece, flip the design to push the glue to the project's inside or back.

That's it! Now you're ready for Halloween!

DIY FLOWER ART NAPKIN RING

Here is a lovely table décor that is worth your time to design. It's so easy to make, you'll want to customize it for a striking effect on your dinner table. Let's make some beautiful napkin rings together.

Required Materials
SVG file for DIY Flower Art Napkin Ring
Cricut Explore machine
12" by 12" StandardGrip mat
Glue
Cricut pens
Cardstock

Instructions

Follow these simple steps to create your own DIY Flower Art Napkin Ring.

Step 1. Download your favorite SVG template > launch Design Space on your computer > upload the template.

Step 2. Spread the template on your cardstock > trace the design with the Cricut pen > transfer the cardstock to the StandardGrip mat.

Step 3. Load the mat into the Cricut machine > pay attention to on-screen draw and cut instructions.

Step 4. Position the napkin rings and glue the edges together.

Voila! Your beautiful napkin rings are done.

3D CANDY CART

A candy cart is a sweet design for someone who loves candy. It can also be a charming, homemade gift for your beloved one. This is suited for a Valentine's Day special gift. Let's see what we need to get started.

Photo via Mandee

Required Materials
Cardstock
SVG template for 3D candy cart
Hot glue
Dura-Lar film
Cricut machine
décorative gems

Instructions

Follow these simple steps to create your own 3D candy cart.

Step 1. Download SVG template for 3D candy art > launch Design Space on your computer > upload the template > send to your Cricut machine.

Step 2. Grab the bottom pieces of the design > fold via the score lines > arrange the wheels, sign, stand, and bottom > apply glue to both wheels and the front sign.

Step 3. Create layers in the oval and scalloped frame pieces > insert the Dura-Lar into the frame pieces > fold the edges and glue the tabs.

Step 4. Arrange the top section pieces > glue the remaining tabs > grab the middle piece > slide the bottom tabs into it > glue the pieces together.

Step 5. Grab the top and bottom pieces > apply the glue > embellish the 3D candy cart with your décorative gems.

How easy was this beautiful project? I hope you enjoyed making it!

3D HOT AIR BALLOON

Asking a beginner crafter to design a 3D air balloon may sound weird, but it's an exciting and fun project that you should give a try. Craft the balloon to add for your home décorations or a friend's house, as it's a great home-made gift idea.

Photo via Mandee

Required Materials
Cardstock
String or kabob sticks
Box
Cricut machine
Hot glue
SVG template for the 3D Hot Air Balloon

Instructions

Follow these simple steps to create your own 3D Hot Air Balloon.

Step 1. Download the SVG template online > launch Design Space on your computer > upload the SVG template > click on Make It.

Step 2. Send the design to your Cricut machine > cut pieces of the 3D hot air balloon.

Step 3. Curl the balloon pieces > fold the tabs inside > glue the balloon strip, top-down > glue the 8 sides together.

Step 4. Curl the top layers and apply glue to the layers > attach each layer on the balloon > add the base décorative pieces > grab the balloon and attach the pieces of the swooping banner, with each banner overlapping the other > add tassel pieces.

Step 5. Grab the box > attach the décorative pieces > fold and attach the tabs > glue the pieces together > use the kabob sticks to clip the balloon to the box.

Just like that, you have a beautiful 3D hot air balloon! Well done!

MINI HALLOWEEN TREAT BAGS

Treat bags can be used all year long, but are vital to have at Halloween. Crafting them is straightforward, yet fun. These treat bags can be customized whichever way you like. Let's get our materials ready and craft these beautiful treat bags.

Photo via Mandee

Required Materials
SVG template for Halloween treat bags
SVG template for Halloween skull
Glue
Vellum
Black vinyl
Cardstock
Cricut machine
Cricut Infusible Ink layering designs

Instructions

Follow these simple steps to create your own mini Halloween treat bag.

Step 1. Download the SVG treat bag and skull templates online or via Cricut Access.

Step 2. Launch Design Space on your computer > upload the templates > set the top of your bag against the images.

Step 3. Click on Contour to create a few pieces of the skull > attach the vinyl with the skull face to form a sticker > craft a rectangle inside the bag for the vellum > adjust the position of the layers and select 'score' > move the project to mat.

Step 4. Attach, cut, shape, and score lines > pay attention to on-screen guidelines to cut pieces of the bag.

Step 5. Arrange the pieces > fold the pieces, following the score lines > place the vellum in the rectangle inside the bag and apply glue > use the skull face to décorate the bag.

Step 6. Grab side and bottom flaps of the bag > apply glue to the flaps.

That's it! Your kids now have home-made treat bags they can show off!

What's your favorite project? We've come a long way! You just got creative with a ton of Cricut projects. From now on, you can design your favorite projects. I hope I inspired you to get started on this creative path. Not to forget, if you're still wondering whether you can make money crafting Cricut projects, jump to the next chapter. Next, you'll learn how to make money with Cricut. See you there!

3

MAKE MONEY WITH CRICUT

Have you ever wondered whether you could make money from crafting? Unique designs sell well when you light the fire of your creativity and create beautiful designs. People appreciate the beautiful results of many of the Cricut projects. You can make tons of money doing what you love! Let's find out how and get you on the way to starting your new business.

Think Outside the Box

Feel free to showcase your creative skills and ingenuity every time you're crafting your designs. At imes, you'll feel like creating something similar to a craft you saw on Amazon, Etsy, or other online marketplaces. That isn't an issue, but what you're crafting shouldn't be a carbon-copy of something you saw online, or you'll have trouble selling your designs.

Thinking outside the box means you are ready to challenge the established order and create a new craft trend. It's not going to be easy winning everyone's trust and confidence. But you're going to be the next hot seller if your idea works! If you create a new craft trend and everyone starts selling it, you're on your way to making lots of money.

However, let's see what thinking outside the box is. You're not expected to come up with designs never heard from before. You are building on existing projects by adding your own style and flair. How do you incorporate my style and flair into a design? Check Etsy, Amazon, and other online marketplaces to see what others are selling and what's popular. Check what these projects have in common and strive to make your own project different.

Make your projects stand out if you're looking for clients to raise your profit margin. Would different fonts make your project look more appealing and enticing? Don't hesitate to change fonts. Always remember that fontbundles.net and other online sources have super deals for premium fonts.

Narrow Your Expertise

Don't try to be a jack of all crafts. Instead, define a personal craft area. Let people know what crafts you do perfectly that other crafters don't. Nobody will trust you to deliver quality designs if you claim to be an expert in all varieties of crafts. Focus on your niche, like crafting shirts, earrings, flowers, and anything else you are good at.

One great mistake Cricut newbies make is crafting everything people ask them to make. When you're crafting everything from birthday t-shirts, tumblers, and home décor, you lose your focus, confuse your customers, and end up wasting your efforts. Instead, opt for one or two projects and master them!

Be Consistent

Consistency is key in every business, and crafting cannot be different. So, if you are going to make money from crafting, you need to make consistency your focus. Don't make crafting something that you do once a month. Do it a few times a week or at least one time a week, as long as you stay consistent. However, the more frequently you practice crafting, the faster you develop your skills and get to make money from your crafts.

Make sure that both your prices and the quality of your designs are consistent to earn the trust of your customers. Do this consistently so that your customers start recommending you to would-be clients.

Don't Give Up

Crafting is a challenging business. You need more than courage to run a successful Cricut business. You've got to develop a never-quit attitude because you're going to face plenty of drawbacks. You will have to cope with days when nothing seems to work, while customers expect great quality!

I wasn't spared drawbacks when I started my crafting business. I emptied my bank account and took loans because I wanted to create as many Cricut projects as possible to sell and make some great money. I'd seen people who sold their crafts and became rich and wanted to be like them. So, I thought if I could create hundreds of projects on my own, I would generate lots of cash in no time. I was wrong!

I made no sales in the first three months. I was hoping that things would work out but creditors kept coming after my assets. Three months became six months, and everything I owned had been taken away from me. I was fast becoming the laughing stock of my neighborhood. I'd already made up my mind to quietly leave the neighborhood and quit crafting.

While I was pondering on the next step to take, a thought struck my mind. *Why are people not buying my crafts?* I wondered. Then, I realized I was busy crafting beautiful projects, but I had not advertised or promoted them at all. I sold over 50 projects the very day that I advertised my designs on my Facebook account.

When challenges pile up, take a deep breath and assure yourself you're up to the task. Only tenacious people can be successful in the Cricut business.

How Much Profit Do You Want?

Determine the amount of profit you really want to make from each project you design. You obviously don't want your price to be so high that your customers will move on. Still, if you fail to consider the cost of materials and sell your designs at a very low price, you're going to be out of business fast.

Value your materials, time, and effort you put into the project before you decide on the price. There's a golden rule for setting a selling price. Multiply the cost of your materials by 2, 3, or 4 to do it. Don't pay attention to people who say you're charging too much. Why? You're an expert in that craft, and you're using the best materials.

People who value quality products will surely patronize you.

Learn a New Thing Daily

Don't allow pride or fear to stop your thirst for knowledge. If there's someone who's experienced in something you don't know, talk to them. You'll need to tap into their experience to understand what's at stake and how you can overcome the challenges of the trade. Don't forget that someone has already designed that craft you're sweating hard to create now. Don't hesitate to contact people who can teach you the tips and tricks of crafting beautiful Cricut projects.

What do I stand to gain by focusing on experienced crafters? Most importantly, they'll give you expert advice on how you can overcome your crafting challenges, create profitable crafts, meet the crafting needs of the customers, and gain customers' trust and confidence.

Reach out to them because they're always ready and willing to help you.

Focus on Quality

Most buyers of Cricut projects admire quality, not quantity. You'll have no issues selling your products if they are top-quality. Let's say you're on Amazon, shopping for a DIY flower art napkin ring. After a few minutes of search, you see two options, one is colorful and vibrant, while the other looks low-quality. Which one would you go for? Sure, nobody would turn down the attractive one. That's how average buyers think.

Always pay attention to how the buyers think. On no condition must you allow your thirst for profit trump the quality of the products you're selling. For example, if the materials for the DIY flower art ring cost you $8 and you're selling each ring for $14, you're doing great. With a profit of $6 per ring and multiple sales per day, you're going to make lots of cash.

Photo via Diana Schröder-Bode

Other crafters may settle for cheaper materials in a desperate bid to beat down your price. Don't panic, even if they're selling their crafts for $4, when you're selling yours for $14. Even when you sell less than they might be, you'll be making more money.

Most customers crave quality products and they're always ready and eager to pay more when they see one. When your customers like the quality of your products, they'll tell their friends to patronize you. You know how crucial word-of-mouth marketing is, don't you?

Licensing and Copyright

Always pay close attention to licensing and copyright laws if you don't want to create legal and financial issues for your budding Cricut business. As you probably already know, stealing another person's intellectual property is considered a crime. Licensing and copyright laws protect peoples' intellectual property. Here, I will walk you through a few Cricut usage policies. If you need legal advice on intellectual property, speak with your lawyer.

- *The Cricut Angel Policy*: Under this policy, you can use images in the Cricut Image Library to create beautiful designs to sell. But make sure you carefully consider the policy to see if it works for you. Just click on this link to read the Cricut Angel policy. The Cricut Angel Policy comes with virtually all Cricut Access images you could think of. With over 10,000 images, you have all you need to create amazing Cricut projects to sell. However, make sure you don't sell individual images or add copyright notices to your Cricut projects. Also, your projects shouldn't use Marvel, Martha Stewart, Disney, or other licensed images.
- *Personal Vs. Commercial Use*: Carefully consider the source of the images you're using for your designs. On no condition should you download images from a search engine just because you want to create projects. If you do, you might be violating copyright laws. Instead, buy your images from online sellers and get familiar with their terms of use. Most purchased images come with personal use licenses. You must not use such images for commercial purposes. But how would you know if you don't read the terms of usage? Having analyzed the terms, you'll know which images come with a commercial license. Obviously, now you know why these terms are so important.
- *Licensed Images*: Online shops often sell images with licensed characters or fonts. Try to avoid such images and fonts if you don't want to get in trouble or break copyright laws. Also, be careful with how you use the licensed images on Cricut

Design Space. Such images cannot be used for commercial purposes. However, feel free to use non-licensed images once you're okay with their Angel Policy. Disclaimer: The author is not qualified to give legal advice and this is just general advice.

PROFITABLE CRICUT PROJECTS TO SELL

Yes, in Chapter Four of this book, you learned some great examples of crafts you could create, sell, and make quite a bit of money on. Below, you get to see details of nine super profitable Cricut projects you can opt for any time, any day.

1. Wall Art: One Cricut project that could fetch you lots of cool cash is the farmhouse wall art. Why? Millions of people search Pinterest and other online outlets for farmhouse wall décor every month. Finding a market or selling your crafted wall décor shouldn't pose any challenge because the demand for these fun-looking artworks is always on the increase.
2. Customized Decals: Cricut end users love customized decals or stickers because they could be used for lots of functions. Big retailers compete with one another on a daily basis for quality personalized stickers. If you're creative enough with your designs, you'll be the go-to crafter for these unique Cricut designs. You know what that means. More crafting orders, more sales, and more profits.
3. Kids' Wall Decals: Kids' events such as birthday parties, baby showers, and baby décors happen throughout the year. Demand for kid-related wall decals will surely be on the increase. Crafting such Cricut projects means you can easily sell your designs. Also, the cost of crafting these kid-friendly projects is bearable.
4. Stickers: Cricut stickers, especially those with shadow layers, are hot on Etsy, Amazon, and other online marketplaces. Planner stickers, like wedding décor, can fetch you lots of cash. The wedding industry is thriving and an average wedding planner craves these lovely Cricut stickers. However, you need to up your crafting skills a bit if you're creating stickers for weddings. Personalize designs if you want to steal the show and grab the attention of couples.
5. Paper Flowers: Lots of buyers comb Etsy and Amazon for paper flowers on a daily basis. Paper flowers have earned an all-time popularity in the marketplace. Pinterest alone sees over a million search requests for paper flowers every month. Paper flowers suit all events, including weddings, birthdays, and specific celebrations, like Mother's Day. You'll surely have lots of sales if you start crafting paper flowers because demand for them is always increasing.
6. Cake and Cupcake Toppers: Some parents are keen to spice up their kids' birthday parties with lots of adorable décor, while others simply want a perfect gift for their kids. Most times, they end up purchasing Cricut cake toppers. These cupcake toppers are cost-effective, but what stands them out is their customized beauty. You'll surely get outstanding patronage if you start crafting these Cricut projects for commercial purposes.
7. Leather Earrings: Craft Cricut leather earrings if you want to sell lots of products. With or without graphic design skills or expertise, you can create and customize charming leather earrings. Make beautiful designs and keep your quality high and buyers will flock to your beautiful jewelry.
8. Felt and Fabric Flowers: Searches for felt and fabric flowers are high. More people are developing a significant interest in these beautiful flowers because they are the perfect

décor for homes and parties. Also, felt and fabric flowers are ideal for various social events. They are also very easy to make.
9. Cards: Crafting Cricut cards are some of the easiest projects to use Cricut for. Besides, cards sell well, and selling them won't cause you sleepless nights. Cards are cost-effective and also suitable for all events, especially birthdays and weddings.

MARKET YOUR CRICUT PROJECTS

Crafting Cricut projects isn't a challenge to most crafters, but marketing these projects can be. But, if that's your major concern now, you shouldn't worry too much. Here are some suggestions that I use for marketing my own projects:

- Word-of-Mouth Marketing: This marketing option sounds traditional, but it's a very powerful method. How does it work? Create beautiful Cricut designs for your friends and loved ones, and ask them to share the projects with their friends on social media. Watch them drive lots of traffic to your online shop or email address. More than likely, some of these people would want to purchase your projects.
- Local Craft Fair: Often, local craft markets are organized for crafters to display, market, and sell their creative artworks. Such markets offer unique opportunities for you to sell your amazing Cricut projects. Just make sure you're taking high-quality products there because you'll be competing with other great crafters.
- Local Pop-up Shops: Open a Craft pop-up shop or look to partner with people with pop-up shops from your area, where you can sell your Cricut projects. You can also get approval to sell your products in schools and worship centers.
- Facebook and Instagram: Feel free to market or sell your Cricut projects via Facebook and Instagram. Why not use your personal Facebook or Instagram page to promote your projects? Doing this means that you get more people to see the crafts you're making and the projects you currently have in stock. Again, apart from your personal Facebook and Instagram pages, you can also use Facebook and Instagram ads to advertise or promote your projects (although you may be charged for this). Lest I forget, Facebook groups can be a potent selling ground for your Cricut projects. Contact the moderator(s) for permission and market your products. Additionally, you can use Twitter the same way.
- Personal Online Shops: Crafters, especially newbies, are encouraged to create an online shop via Etsy, WooCommerce, Shopify, Square Space, eBay, Amazon, or other online marketplaces. An account on these platforms will help you to showcase the comparative advantages of your projects, as well as to market and sell them. Which of these online shops is more suitable for my Cricut projects?

1. Shopify: Information retrieved via their website shows that you can use the platform to sell your products to anyone worldwide through POS, social media, or other online marketplaces. Create an account on the platform, launch your dashboard, and manage orders, payments, and shipping. Over one million businesses across 175 countries have recorded more than 200 billion USD in sales via Shopify.
2. eBay: Lots of sellers are using eBay to promote and market their products. Like Shopify, you can sell your products to anyone around the world using the marketplace.
3. SquareSpace: Based on what they explain on their site, SquareSpace is the right place

to be if you want to customize your online store or grow your craft business. With lots of SEO tools, the platform is gradually becoming the choice of most businesses.
4. WooCommerce: Opt for WooCommerce if all you want is to create the eCommerce platform of your dreams. You surely can use this new online marketplace to promote your products and boost your sales.
5. Etsy: Sell your Cricut projects in Etsy, a reputable online marketplace. It is actually a unique global market where hundreds of thousands of people transact business on a daily basis. However, your privacy is strongly protected.
6. Amazon: Create an account with Amazon Handmade to join their league of artisan sellers. The account has to be approved before you can sell your products via the platform. However, once your application for account creation is approved, you get a waiver for the Professional Selling fee. Currently, artisans from over 90 countries around the world sell their handmade crafts via Amazon. Amazon is considered a community of successful craft businesses.

Feel free to create an account on all these online marketplaces if you believe you need all of them to market your business. I would suggest you pick only two options that serve your needs best. This way, you can easily monitor the business and attend to the needs of your customers on time. There are also mobile app versions for all these online marketplaces. So, depending on the device you're using, you can always get the app via the Google Store or Apple Store.

CONCLUSION

Cricut Project and Profit Ideas for 2021 and Beyond: The Beginner's Step-by-Step Guide to Tons of Project Ideas and Making Money Fast with Cricut is a three-chapter book with lots of tricks on how you can make money crafting lovely projects with your Cricut machine.

The book addressed several core Cricut issues including details on the finest and most profitable Cricut projects to create and sell. Now that you're done reading the book, you're likely a pro crafter if you tried your hand at all the projects.

Chapter One addressed Cricut project ideas and their materials. There, the emphasis was placed on the right materials for specific Cricut projects. For ease of reference, these materials were grouped under five categories: paper crafting ideas, vinyl craft project ideas, heat transfer project ideas, fabric craft ideas, and Cricut infusible ink project ideas. Several project examples were listed under each category. Also, the chapter listed the finest Cricut crafts you could create, sell, and start earning money on!

Chapter Two provided a step-by-step guide for crafting unique Cricut projects. There, you learned a few tricks on how to create complete projects, such as a DIY greeting card, DIY label, vinyl on mugs, Iron-On t-shirt, and Iron-On Adoption banner. You also learned to design paper butterfly hearts, Infusible ink layered t-shirts, DIY giant paper flowers, DIY Valentine's wreaths, and cupcake wrappers with flowers. Even more projects taught you to make spider web garlands, DIY flower art napkin rings, 3D candy carts, 3D hot air balloons, and mini Halloween treat bags.

Finally, Chapter Three delved much into how to up your creativity to design beautiful Cricut projects that bring you a profit. You learned a few Cricut projects that sell well and how to market your Cricut projects.

It's time to take action on what you've learned. Go ahead to create your favorite Cricut projects. You've got the right crafting tools and tricks, and there's nothing left to be afraid of!

290 | CONCLUSION

Please leave me a review on Amazon if you really enjoyed reading this book. Your support is greatly appreciated.

REFERENCES

Abbi Kirsten Collections (2016, May 13). Easy Method When Building any DIY Giant Paper Flower.

https://www.abbikirstencollections.com/2016/05/easy-method-when-building-any-diy-giant-paper-flower.html?fbclid=IwAR1Zj_TThB-fTn0M618nC1QmdMXULBHJET5HhY96IqnEbCu03P1CRn5gxFw

Amazon (N. D). Cricut project images. Https://Amazon.com

Bethadilly (2020, April 14). Cupcake toppers with a Cricut: A Quick and Easy Guide.

https://youtu.be/TClLMOOyq70

Blackstone, C. (2018, August 26). Making some spiderweb garland for Halloween using Design Space and Cricut. https://youtu.be/GhAOspy6n-8

Coco, B. (2015, May 17). Crochet: How to crochet a coaster.

https://www.google.com/url?sa=t&source=web&rct=j&url=https://m.youtube.com/watch%3Fv%3DIum6UBEEpm0&ved=2ahUKEwi2q9Sp56DvAhXpQxUIHcoPB3IQ28sGMAF6BAgBECI&usg=AOvVaw2oVd8o1sxvx8o_lEAU4S3E

Color made Happy (N.D). Easy Cricut Joy keychain project.

https://colormadehappy.com/easy-cricut-joy-keychain-project/

Daily Dose of DIY with Chris (2020, April 1). Make Easy Greeting Cards with Cricut.

https://youtu.be/HXYMoCQL6gI

REFERENCES

Day Dream into Reality (2020, August 12). DIY personalized Cricut socks. https://www.daydreamintoreality.com/cricut-socks/

Dennis, C. (2020, March 12). What Is A Cricut Machine And What Does It Do? https://thediymommy.com/what-is-a-cricut-machine-and-what-does-it-do/

Designs by Miss Mandee (2021, January 7). Woven Baskets - Die Cut Baskets. https://www.designsbymissmandee.com/2021/01/woven-baskets/

Designs by Miss Mandee (2021, January 13). 3D Hot Air Balloon. https://www.designsbymissmandee.com/2021/01/3d-hot-air-balloon/

Designs by Miss Mandee (2021, January 27). 3D Valentine Candy Cart: Valentine's Day Cut file. https://www.designsbymissmandee.com/2021/01/3d-valentine-candy-cart/

Etsy (N.D). Leather hair accessories. https://www.etsy.com/market/leather_hair_accessories

George, C. (2019, July 22). How to Use the Cricut Maker Debossing Tool. https://heyletsmakestuff.com/cricut-maker-debossing-tool/

George C. (2019, August 5). How to Use the Cricut Maker Perforation Tool.https://heyletsmakestuff.com/cricut-maker-perforation-tool/

George, M. (2020, February 13). Cricut Joy – What Can It Do & How Does It Work? https://www.polishedhabitat.com/cricut-joy/

Goldwyn, B. (2019, June 21). The Ultimate Guide to Using the Cricut Maker's Knife Blade to Cut
Wood. https://www.bybrittanygoldwyn.com/using-the-cricut-knife-blade-to-cut-wood/

Hometalk (2018, March 25). DIY Hack to Make Labels with Packing tape. https://images.app.goo.gl/14QwjM9GpGiBJnJR9

Jennifer Maker (2019, June 4). How to Make a t-shirt with a Cricut. https://jennifermaker.com/make-t-shirt-cricut/

Jennifer Maker (2019, June 14). Cricut infusible ink layered t-shirt tutorial. https://youtu.be/XB5fl98d2FU

Jennifer Maker (2018, December 14). How to put vinyl on mugs + cute designs & a unicorn!

REFERENCES | 293

https://jennifermaker.com/vinyl-on-mugs-cute-designs/

Jennifer Maker (2019, February 3). DIY Paper Butterfly Canvass Wall Heart on Cricut.

https://jennifermaker.com/paper-butterfly-canvas-wall-art-heart/

Kayla's Cricut Creations (2019, February 2). How to make paper flowers with Cricut.

https://www.google.com/url?sa=t&source=web&rct=j&url=https://m.youtube.com/watch%3Fv%3DSsD_M8jLG6o&ved=2ahUKEwjbpLiDkZnvAhXcQhUIHYsxDu4Q28sGMAB6BAgBEAc&usg=AOvVaw2SIqH8FgsyOU_SBoacyaH

Kundin, H. (N.D). The Cricut Maker Machine – What's New and What Can It Do?

https://www.happinessishomemade.net/the-cricut-maker-machine-whats-new-and-what-can-it-do/

Kundin, H. (N.D). How to Use the Cricut Maker Engraving Tool.

https://www.happinessishomemade.net/cricut-maker-engraving-tool/

Makers Gonna Learn (N.D). Easy Holiday Napkin Rings with Cricut. https://youtu.be/wbyggCN_7aI

Paper Luv (2020, December 30). Valentine's Day Heart Wreath Wall.

https://youtu.be/J_i5W6EmWBA

Purin, M. (N.D). Gingerbread Centerpiece. Unsplash.

https://unsplash.com/s/photos/gingerbread-centerpiece

Runyan, S. (N.D). DIY Custom Backpack.

https://www.google.com/url?sa=t&source=web&rct=j&url=https://m.youtube.com/watch%3Fv%3DKYowNgyKlsA&ved=2ahUKEwjqmf2EtKDvAhV4UhUIHUsFC4gQ28sGMAl6BAgsEAc&usg=AOvVaw15i3Pxr_wQY_yjPswN52H4

The Flower Art (2017, December 14). Easy DIY: How to Make Felt Roses.

https://www.google.com/url?sa=t&source=web&rct=j&url=https://m.youtube.com/watch%3Fv%3DCrpu-1i_8aY&ved=2ahUKEwj8p7K54qDvAhXgShUIHSaQCJMQ28sGMAx6BAg1EBM&usg=AOvVaw2AB0XJ8GCvlBBSq_xNzeTB

Printed in Great Britain
by Amazon